GOLDEN GATE SEMINARY LIBRARY

What Jesus Means to Me

ABOUT THE AUTHORS

Emmanuel Lemuel McCall, Sr., is associate secretary in the Department of Work with National Baptists of the Southern Baptist Home Mission Board.

Robert H. Wilson is pastor of St. John Baptist Church, Dallas, Texas.

Percy A. Carter, Jr., is pastor of Hosack Street Baptist Church, Columbus, Ohio.

Nelson H. Smith, Jr., is pastor of New Pilgrim Baptist Church, Birmingham, Alabama.

Charles E. Boddie is president of American Baptist Theological Seminary, Nashville, Tennessee.

Edward V. Hill is pastor of Mount Zion Missionary Baptist Church, Los Angeles, California.

Manuel L. Scott is pastor of Calvary Baptist Church, Los Angeles, California.

SEVEN BLACK PREACHERS TELL

WHAT JESUS MEANS TO ME

BROADMAN PRESS
Nashville, Tennessee

© Copyright 1971 · Broadman Press
All rights reserved
422 –16
ISBN: 0–8054–2216–1

Library of Congress Catalog Card Number: 76–178068
Dewey Decimal Classification: 248.2
Printed in the United States of America

PREFACE

Part of the objective of Broadman Press is the publishing of books that "help persons in the areas of personal faith, personality development, character growth, and human relations." In fulfilling this objective, inspirational books from Broadman strive always to hold up Jesus Christ, for, ultimately, Jesus is the central message of a Christian publisher. A Christian never tires of hearing about his Lord. In the words of the treasured hymn: "Every day with Jesus is sweeter than the day before." It is always fitting for Christians to share with one another what Jesus means to each.

Therefore Broadman asked the preachers you will meet in the following pages to share with you a simple testimony on ground common to all Christians. In the welter of words on the secular market there is much about and by Black Christians; we felt that someone should report simple testimonies; regardless of the sociological implications of the Black experience in America, there seems value in sharing the love of Jesus—this is not the task of the secular press, but it is our assignment.

Naturally, the testimonies given herein are those of the authors. Views expressed are neither necessarily in agreement with nor in conflict with the views of Broadman Press nor of the Southern Baptist Convention. Writers were asked to speak as they felt led; and they are presented herein as they spoke.

There is no particular significance in the choice of the persons nor in the arrangement of the chapters. We asked a number of Black preachers at random; these were the seven who responded.

On behalf of Broadman Press I would like to express personal appreciation to the writers of the following chapters for their gracious cooperation.

An Appendix carries short biographical information concerning the authors.

WILLIAM CANNON
Editor, Inspirational Books
Broadman Press

CONTENTS

1 EMMANUEL LEMUEL MC CALL, SR.
I FIND CHRIST THROUGH RELATIONSHIPS   11

2 ROBERT H. WILSON
WHAT JESUS MEANS TO ME   29

3 PERCY A. CARTER, JR.
BEING BORN ALIVE TO SERVE   47

4 NELSON H. SMITH, JR.
WHAT JESUS MEANS TO ME   65

5 CHARLES E. BODDIE
WHAT JESUS CHRIST MEANS TO ME   79

6 EDWARD V. HILL
WHAT CHRIST MEANS TO ME   99

7 MANUEL L. SCOTT
WHAT JESUS MEANS TO ME   113

CONTRIBUTORS   127

1
Emmanuel Lemuel McCall, Sr.
I FIND CHRIST THROUGH RELATIONSHIPS

The essence of my spiritual pilgrimage has been finding Christ in the lives of others. This is not to say that I have a vicarious or lecherous faith. Nor is it to minimize my own commitment to Jesus Christ. It is to say that I was lead to Christ by the relationships which those around had with him, and I have found spiritual sustenance in fellowship with other believers.

I cannot say when my spiritual pilgrimage began. Perhaps during infancy as I was carried to and from the church house by my parents: certainly during my nursery and preschool years as Annie Dobbs and Mary Office did their utmost to impart their knowledge of God. These were not exceptionally trained women; just ordinary. They gathered us together in that one-room church at Wheatland, Pennsylvania, and led us to the choir stand; that's where the preschoolers met.

There are two vivid recollections which I have of those years. One was the frustrated anticipation of being able to reach the floor with my feet rather than dangling them in midair. The other was the recitation period each Sunday. In our little church each class gave a review of the lesson. The remembrance of standing on the raised portion of the auditorium, in a line, singing songs and saying by rote what had been drilled into us, is still a golden memory. My academic training since then has suggested that this was not the way to do it, but these ladies didn't know this. They were doing the best they could, and I am sure they were a part of my pilgrimage.

I cannot say when my spiritual pilgrimage began. Perhaps with the various influences in our home. Both of my parents were and are Christian. Dad was adopted by the minister of our church during his early teens. He was not originally a Pennsylvanian. He was born and grew up in Cheraw, South Carolina, but at an early age the patterns of segregation forced him to seek refuge outside of Cheraw and vicinity. Dad was taken in and adopted by the Reverend Samuel DeLane. Reverend DeLane too was a vital part of our home.

During those early years we moved two or three times, and I can recall Sam DeLane dedicating each house we moved to. When we moved to the farm where Mom and Dad still live, there was the Reverend DeLane, dedicating the house. Often he came by either to fill a five-gallon glass jar with well water which he used for dietary problems, or to gather wild greens and herbs, or just to look in on his "children." There was always a bag of candy from his store which accompanied each visit. Reverend DeLane operated a grocery store in the nearby town called Farrell. And then on Christmas there was usually a large bag of fruit, nuts, and candy. These gifts were only incidental, however, to the presence and personality of our spiritual leader.

It would be unfair to say that Dad picked up all of his spiritual heritage from Samuel DeLane. He came to Pennsylvania with a firm faith already established. One of my continuing remembrances of Dad is his singing while he worked. The reason I remembered his singing is that he did not usually sing the songs we sang in church. In church we sang songs from the *Baptist Standard Hymnal*. The songs he sang were the mournful songs begun during the slave era and nurtured in the many experiences that the Negro has faced in America. They were mournful in tune yes, but they reflected a hope. They bore a testimony of God's continuing care and concern for his deprived and despised children. Dad learned these

I Find Christ Through Relationships

songs in South Carolina, but he kept singing them in Pennsylvania.

Both of my parents have been active Bible students and have spent many years teaching in the church school activities of the Valley Baptist Church. I am sure that my spiritual pilgrimage has had some relationship to their Bible study and discussions at home or to the many church folks who often came to our home and our visits to theirs.

I cannot say when my spiritual pilgrimage began. Perhaps my grandmother, my mother's mother had some influence. She belonged to the "prayer band." This was a group of women who met weekly at various homes for prayer services. These prayer services were just that. Nothing but singing and praying, then crying and sometimes shouting. As a child it used to scare me to hear the shouting, but I learned to expect it from certain women and to even be able to predict the eruption by the progression of emotional build-up. We children, there were three of us often had to accompany Granny to the "prayer bands." This most often came when she cared for us during my mother's frequent sick spells. Mom had a serious problem with asthma during our childhood years.

My grandmother is not a learned woman. She is very ordinary, but it is that simple, trusting faith that has been an inspiration to me. She is of Cherokee Indian background which is very evident from the moment you look at her, but she never seemed "Indian" to me (as a child) because she always lived above the "Indian" image that we learned from the cowboy pictures. She was a Christian. The imagery of the motion picture savage and my Christian grandmother could never coalesce. She taught me indirectly what it means to trust God.

I cannot say when my spiritual pilgrimage began, but I do know when I made known my public commitment to follow Jesus. It was on the first Sunday of June, 1941, that this five-year-old boy came up to his father during the interval between Sunday School and morning worship. "Daddy, I want to join the church." Dad was baffled, I'm sure. The only thing he knew to say was, "Go see your grandpa." This, of course, was the Reverend DeLane of whom I spoke earlier. I can recall bouncing over to Grandpa with my same expression. "Grandpa, I want to join the church." He then took me to an anteroom on the side of the choir stand which served as his study. For about five minutes he questioned me. When he was satisfied, he instructed me as to the proper time in the service to make this known.

My public commitment did not come as a result of great clamour or struggle or soul searching. A five-year-old logically should have had none of these. It was the simple desire of a child who had learned about Jesus through other relationships, to want that same Jesus for himself. And this is perhaps the key to my own pilgrimage, even to the present. Christ has been most real to me in human relationships rather than moments of personal piety. A devotional life of prayer, meditation, and Bible study has always had a place in my life, but those peaks of spiritual mountaintops have not come in moments of isolation. They have come in relationships to others.

I know that one of the continuing controversial questions among churchmen is whether or not a five-year-old can have a valid Christian experience. I cannot speak for anyone else, but I do know that Emmanuel Lemuel McCall had a valid experience of commitment at age five. Oh yes, there have been times of doubt. At least twice in my life I questioned the validity of my initial conversion experience. One of those times was very traumatic. let me tell you about it.

I had made a public statement concerning my call to the ministry at age fourteen. Reverend Frank James Waller who was then minister of the Valley Baptist Church requested that the church license me to preach immediately upon the hearing of a trial sermon. His philosophy was that a preacher is trained by being in relationship to preachers and preaching. So on November 21, 1950, at 3:00 P.M. the Valley Baptist Church family assembled to hear this fourteen-year-old "boy preacher." I was granted a license to preach immediately thereafter.

I Find Christ Through Relationships

But it was during the next spring when we were holding revival services that the guest speaker initiated my spiritual trauma. For ten successive nights I heard this man, in various ways, some subtle and otherwise, suggest that if you did not see certain signs or have certain feelings then you weren't saved. Needless to say, I had experienced none of his feelings nor had I seen any of his "signs." I came away convinced that I was not saved. But now I was embarrassed. How does a preacher come down out of a pulpit (in the Negro church all preachers sit on the pulpit) and make a profession of faith.

Well the anxiety and trauma continued until July of my fifteenth year. The only thing I knew to do was to go forward on the next baptizing Sunday. This I did to the complete amazement and bewilderment of everyone. When Reverend Waller came out of the pulpit and heard my request, his only statement was, "You are old enough to know what you are doing. Go back and get dressed for the water."

That afternoon I discovered that the spiritual trauma was still with me. Perhaps it was now compounded by embarrassment. It was something that continued to haunt me after I left Wheatland, Pennsylvania, and was a freshman at the University of Louisville.

During this time the second wave of doubt, a carry-over from that first experience, had obsessed me. I was helped through informal conversation around a Ping-Pong table. I discovered that there were other students having similar doubts and misgivings. Fred Witty, our BSU director was wise enough to observe that at least two of us had been unduly influenced by "super-Christians" trying to play God and making their experiences normative for all. I never have forgotten his statement: "Some people need to be knocked down and dragged out. Unless God does some unusual things with them, they never will see the light. But some of us can find God without all of that." Since that time that element of doubt has never again dampened my spirits. No longer am I compelled to accept any man's experiences as the norm for my own life.

I have already alluded to my call to the ministry. As early as age eight, I was aware of God's claim on me to the ministry of preaching. It was only an awareness. During my thirteenth year I became more preoccupied with the ministry as a vocation. I had been constantly exposed to preachers. Not only had Reverend DeLane been a frequent visitor in our home and on the farm, but after him was Reverend A. H. Hunter and Reverend Frank J. Waller. We had a farm, and my parents were naturally generous towards preachers. This often included freely giving produce to not only our pastors but also their friends. I remember at various times since that eighth year having said that I was going to preach when I grew up. Those who knew me casually began to refer to me as such.

Following the evening service on the second Sunday in October, 1950, I went up to Reverend Waller and announced my desire to preach. He, of course, rejoiced and informed my parents. The seven-mile ride from the church in Wheatland to the farm was a quiet one. After we got home, the only thing that Dad could say was, "Why didn't you tell us first?" I don't know why and have never tried to psychoanalyze myself to find out. My parents, however, were delighted with my decision and have done everything one could do to facilitate my development. In fact my first preacher's suit happened to have been my dad's. Since age fourteen, we have been the same height and generally the same weight. At the time of my trial sermon most preachers wore black. So I delivered my trial sermon in Dad's black suit, with his black tie and my black shoes.

One of the greatest blessings to my ministerial development have been those with whom I have been in relationship. In addition to the loving care of my family, there was the Reverend Frank James Waller. Every preacher whom I have ever met that knew him called him a preacher's friend. He took a special interest in me partly because I was young, partly because I was a member of his church, but especially because I fulfilled a void in his life. Frank

I Find Christ Through Relationships

Waller had always wanted "a son to give back to the Lord, but since I had only five girls the Lord gave me you." He always treated me as a son. I accompanied him on pastoral visits, I sat in on committee meetings, I conducted the worship and assisted in funerals, I accompanied him to convention meetings. I especially liked the convention meetings because Frank Waller never considered me in his way. Even though he relished the meeting of old friends and acquaintances, I was made to feel as important as anyone else.

But he taught me. Not in a formal sense, but informally, casually, by example. I learned from Frank Waller to appreciate beauty, quality, and godliness. I learned protocol, ethics, sermonic techniques, parliamentary procedures and rhetoric, the techniques of debate. That which I may have learned from him was reinforced by the quality of ministerial friends and associates he had. Two of these men are worth mentioning.

One of these is the Reverend Dr. Jesse L. McFarland. Jesse was a young man then pastoring in New Castle, Pennsylvania. He was and is a skilful athlete, a preacher of unusual ability, and a man of great wisdom. During these formative years Jesse McFarland offered many opportunities to facilitate my development. I often supplied in his church. He, too, helped me understand human development and psychology. Yet the thing which I remember Dr. McFarland most for is the honesty with which he helped me work through the mistakes of my immaturity. Like Frank Waller he could be sympathetically blunt. No wishy-washiness. No hesitation. I never felt hurt after chastisement from either of these men. Helped, yes. Hurt, never. But I learned from being in relationship to them.

The second man whose association with Frank Waller was of personal help to me was Reverend Arvel Carrol. At age seventeen I went to Louisville, Kentucky, to attend Simmons Bible College. Reverend Waller had attended Simmons when it was a full-fledged university, prior to the disaster of the 1930's. He wanted me to attend Simmons for the doctrinal discipline of the late Dr. Marshall B. Lanier. But I also left Pennsylvania with instructions to look up Reverend Arvel Carroll. When I arrived in Louisville, I was immediately impressed with Dr. Jesse V. Bottoms, the acting dean of Simmons. I was equally impressed with the friendliness and warmth of the Green Street Baptist Church which he pastored. So the first year and a half of my Louisville stay was spent in that church.

In January, 1955, I finally got around to visiting the Reverend Arvel Carroll at the Joshua Tabernacle Baptist Church. Here was a man of limited educational training because he had to start late in life. But he was a very warmhearted, open man whose humility overwhelmed you. In his church study he talked with me at length about the dreams and aspirations which he had for Joshua Tabernacle, and then he persuaded me to consider coming to his church as an associate.

Reluctantly I shared my decision with J. V. Bottoms but was encouraged by his vision of greater possibilities for service and development at Joshua Tabernacle. "I have other associates here. Your opportunities of development would be limited. Brother Carroll has no associate. You can help him and he will help you."

With this matter settled, I joined the Joshua Tabernacle Baptist Church. I never have regretted that decision. At Joshua I learned what it means to relate to people whose dreams and desires have been thwarted at various stages of life—people who were powerless to change the conditions, but had learned how to live victorious amidst the odds. To use an overused expression, these people had "soul." This was a new dimension for me.

Reverend Carroll allowed me an unusual amount of latitude in reshaping the educational activities of the church. Beyond these responsibilities I often supplied in the pulpit and carried out other pastoral duties. I made mistakes, but they were learning mistakes. I was at times insensitive to the needs and aspirations of the people. I was sometimes caught up in dreams that were detached from reality. Both pastor and people tolerated and forgave my im-

I Find Christ Through Relationships

maturity and helped me grow in my ability to relate to people.

Perhaps the most leveling remembrances of Joshua Tabernacle has been the development of relationships. I learned from people who had little or no formal training but who had observed well the lessons of life and were wise. I learned from those who were skilled and professional. Even now I rejoice at the opportunities to be in their presence. I did not cease to find Christ in relationships.

I have found Christ even in the relationships of my wife's family who were members of Joshua. Marie and I dated during my college days. She was one of the organists there. On the same day that I graduated from the University of Louisville (I stayed at Simmons only one year and then transferred to the University of Louisville.), we were married at the Joshua Tabernacle Baptist Church. During those years of courtship I found Christ in the relationship of Marie's family. I had always found warmth and acceptance in my many, many visits. If the continued presence of a college student at Sunday dinner was an annoyance, I never knew it. Now that we are family, a Christian perspective does not cease to be the substance of our relationships. I have continued to find Christ in our marriage. Marie could not be the gracious kind of preacher's wife that she is without the discipline of his spirit. Christ with us is not optioned or enforced, he is just there. When he is there, no gimmicks are needed, no promotion is called for. You just be yourself.

I have found Christ in other relationships. I have found him in Southern Seminary. Marie and I lived in both Judson and Rice Halls, B.R. (before remodeling). We were on campus just as the civil rights movement was in full swing (1959–1963). As could be expected, we found the gamut of reactions from interest, to empathy, to sympathy, to resentment and even some hate stares. The latter was the unusual. Ninety-nine and one-half percent of our experiences were enjoyable ones. Here we were with students who for the first time found the freedom to break out of the traditional molds. They wanted the opportunities to know Negroes. They sought us out as a means of filling the void in their own experience and for overcoming the handicaps of their past. The seminary community encouraged this kind of openness. At that time we were the only Negro couple on campus. Responding to the various social invitations was taxing, but we saw it as a ministry. As a consequence, there are many friendships which we have sustained from our seminary experiences. Many doors of opportunity have been occasioned by those friendships.

Very nostalgic to us has been the memory of our friendship with John and Marie Gleason. We had adjoining apartments on the third floor of Rice Hall. On August 23, 1960, Marie and I had dressed to go out to celebrate our second wedding anniversary. Just as we were leaving our apartment the Gleasons were leaving theirs. We teased each other about being "dressed-up" and then began comparing notes. We discovered that we were all going out for the same reason, to celebrate a wedding anniversary. But what was more interesting was that we were married on the same day and same year. We arrived at Niagara Falls at the same time, even though they drove from Virginia and we drove from Kentucky. We stayed at the same motel at Niagara for about the same length of time. Finding these notes of commonality about ourselves deepened our friendship. The patterns of segregation limited the number of things we could do together outside of the seminary community. But there were other things we could do, and we did.

I have found Christ in my relationships of service. For almost eight years I pastored the Twenty-eighth Street Baptist Church in Louisville. A small church, yes, but it was what I needed to continue developing for meaningful service. There were some rough edges in my own personality that needed trimming. This happened through the discipline that Twenty-eighth Street offered. I went there after my first year in the seminary. One of my most rewarding experiences has been to see that church grow. It grew during my presence but even more so since I left.

I Find Christ Through Relationships

During those years Christ became more real as we grew together spiritually. Since photography is a hobby of mine, I began taking 8 mm movies for my first year. These movies cataloged the significant events in the life of the church during my pastorate. It has been interesting to see the growth in size of the children, to see the progression of developments but also to remember the joys and struggles, the times of misunderstanding and weeping, but more especially the times of healing and health. As I reviewed these scenes, occasionally I remember special moments of crisis that occurred with various ones. There were the usual sicknesses, domestic troubles, family and personal problems, incidents of psychosis, and death. Especially while looking again at those who have died have I been refreshed by remembrances of their lives and the incidents of their death.

There are three people in the congregation to whom I am especially indebted because of what they contributed to my spiritual development.

There was Stout Bird, a man whose wisdom had enabled him to retire from four jobs but a man who is deep in piety, rich in wisdom, and whose heart is open in mercy. Whenever there were tasks to be done either on the church property or in the extension of its ministry, there was Stout Bird. But he was also of help in steadying the ambitiousness of the young pastor. Often I wanted to get things done in a hurry. Stout offered the necessary drag to keep me and the church from acting unwisely or doing things that would have to be redone.

I can never forget the time when we purchased the fencing around the lot of the old Emmanuel Baptist Church. The church building was relocated and the old property was purchased by Urban Renewal. Through the intercession of Stout Bird we were able to purchase for $25 the chain link fencing and posts that Emmanuel Baptist Church had paid more than $800 for. Stout Bird led a crew of retired men from our church to go up, take the fence down, dig up the posts, and knock off the three-feet casing of concrete that had anchored them. I felt guilty about Stout Bird, Robert Beck, Tillman Blackman, and Robert Anderson, all retired, and all elderly doing this strenuous work. I felt so guilty that I skipped afternoon classes at the seminary and went to help. I picked up the five-pound sledgehammer and started on the concrete. After about ten strokes, I was out of wind. Stout Bird walked over and said, "Brother Pastor let me have it for a while. You need a rest." With techniques taught by experience, he and Robert Beck succeeded with amazing accuracy in removing the fence and posts and relocating them on our church property.

With all of these men and the other deacons as well, I found Christ in the fellowship of our relations. Whether we were involved in the numerous work projects, at leisure, at recreation, in service or in worship, I found Christ in these men.

The other two people of which I spoke were husband and wife, Julius and Sina Harris. Sina was registrar at Simmons Bible College. I was serving on the faculty there as I did for ten years while also pastoring Twenty-eighth Street Baptist Church. It was through Sina that I was contacted by the pulpit committee and later called to the church.

I think of this couple as I do of the relationship existing between Apollos, Aquila, and Priscilla (Acts 18:24–28). It was their keenness of perception that caused me to continually reexamine my pronouncements from the pulpit and my ideas about what church was all about.

It is not unusual for us in the pulpit to assume that because of divine appointment we have all of the answers. We must also remember that we are human and capable of human errors in judgment and thinking. It was always a consolation to know that I could depend on Sina and J. C. to level with me, but always in the spirit of love. We were not in competition; we were allies in the same cause. I found Christ in my relationships with them.

Before leaving my Louisville experiences I should mention one other. I have found Christ as a result of professional competition.

I Find Christ Through Relationships

I had served as an associate at Joshua Tabernacle some six years before going to Twenty-eighth Street Baptist Church. Two years after I left Joshua Tabernacle, Pastor Carroll had a brain stroke which left him incapacitated. After a two-year recovery period, he retired. Joshua Tabernacle considered two men at the same time in establishing a choice for successor. The two were James Snardon and myself. Both of us had been members of the church. Jim acknowledged his calling to the ministry out of that church, in fact he preached his initial sermon on the Sunday after I was married in August, 1958.

I had just assumed, as did others, that because I had already completed college and two seminary degrees, plus having had some 13 years preaching and pastoral experience over him that I would be called. The congregation felt otherwise. Jim was unanimously called. No politics were involved. Just the moving of God's Spirit.

For some reason or another there was a general assumption that Jim and I would become bitter enemies. We had previously only been casual friends. Just the opposite of what was expected happened. Rather than becoming enemies we and our families have become the best of friends. While I was in Louisville our churches worshiped together and carried on joint ministries. The Snardons and my family have often vacationed together, and even though now separated by miles, no more than three weeks have elapsed when we have not communicated by phone.

The Snardons were not the only close friends we left in Louisville. There were Thurmond and Cora Coleman, Clarence and Charles Etta Lucas, the William H. Sullivans, the William Rodgers, and the John R. Claypools. But our relationship with Jim and Mary Francis Snardon grew out of crisis. In that crisis we found Christ.

Well I'm in Atlanta, Georgia, now, and I have found Christ in my relationships here. I have found him in Reverend James A. Wilborn and the Union Baptist Church. We came to Atlanta, hating to leave our friends in Louisville, scared because of all of the stories we had heard about life in the deep South, uncertain because of the change from the pastorate to denominational service. Our period of adjustment was made easy because of our pastor and our church. Our church is a warm fellowship, although predominately Negro it is multiracial.

Marie has found fulfilment in the music program and the friendships she has formed. I have found satisfaction not only in the church fellowship but most especially in my relationship with my pastor. J. A. Wilborn is still considered a young man, although his oldest son is a seminarian. He has used me freely for much pulpit supply and for assisting in pastoral functions when necessary. I have been awed by the complete trust that this man would put in one who was a total stranger. Through J. A. Wilborn's trust, I have found Christ in him.

I have found Christ in my secretary, Mrs. Mary Leach. How does a young, white women tell her relatives and friends, in Georgia, that she is secretary to a Negro? In our social activities outside of the Home Mission Board building it does take courage and grace to live down the stares and snide remarks that come from those who cannot stand to see black and white together. In this woman I have found not only secretarial competence, but also the kind of maturity which is needed to cope with an area as sensitive as mine is, developing better race relations. Her attitude has been reflected in her competence. Both have made my tasks a lot easier. I am sure that it is the person of Christ in her that helps her to be what she is. I have found Christ in her.

I have found Christ in our other relationships here at the Board. I have found him in my colleagues Victor Glass and Wendell Grigg, men who have given their lives in helping Southern Baptists change their attitudes about race. I have found Christ in Dr. Arthur Rutledge, the Executive Secretary of the Home Mission Board, who sensing the need to have a Negro related to this ministry was willing to run the risk of criticism and scorn that has certainly come. I have found Christ in the support and freedom

I Find Christ Through Relationships

which I have in fulfilling my tasks.

More especially, I have found Christ in the people who attend Southern Baptist churches and institutions. It is unfortunate that only the negative and the notorious make the headlines. For this reason some outside of the Southern Baptist Convention circles assume that all Southern Baptists are bigots and racists. My experiences have shown that there are many who "have never bowed the knee to Baal." Others who had previously bowed to the false god "segregation" are helping to hasten his demise. They are embarrassed over the past, yes, but are doing their best to right the wrongs of history. Because they have yielded themselves to the lordship of Christ and are at least trying to be fully committed, I can do no less than to keep continued relationship with them in our struggle.

Some of my Negro brethren, some in other church groups, even the press have repeatedly asked me, "Why do you tie yourself to Southern Baptists considering what they have been?" My answer comes from my relationship to Christ. If Christ were to relate himself to us because of what we were, who amongst us could be saved? Thanks be to God, he judges us according to what we are and what we can become. I am committed to Southern Baptists because of who they are, but more especially what they can become. This can only be done through relationships—Christ's, theirs, and mine.

2 WHAT JESUS MEANS TO ME
Robert H. Wilson

In my very earliest recognition of awareness, I knew that I *was* a preacher! Though that was quite ambitious at the time of my early childhood, it nevertheless colored and in large measure determined my total experience. There has been no time in my life since my self-awareness that I have not cherished the privilege of preaching the glorious gospel of our Lord, Jesus Christ!

My mother, the late Ida Ellison Wilson, was a simple God-fearing woman. Though there were no preachers in my family, she told me that I began my "preaching" effort almost coevally with my beginning to talk at the age of three. While I do not actually remember the very first efforts, I do clearly recall my "preaching" the three or four years before my first sermon in a church. My siblings and the neighborhood children comprised my congregation, and any creek bank or yard was the church. I even recall the title of my "sermon" so often used (which, in fact, variously stated was the entire sermon.): "Turn your back on the devil and your face to the Lord." I also recall the Sunday afternoon when I and my entire congregation spilled through the neighborhood in tears after our "service" on the creek bank had disturbed the worship of the local church and its pastor threatened all of us with hell's fire.

I was nine years old when I preached for the first time in a church. The Little Zion Baptist Church of my native Columbia,

South Carolina, was a neighborhood storefront. Although I cannot recall the pastor's name, I do remember that he extended my first preaching experience to a two-week revival when the neighborhood expressed interest in hearing the "boy preacher." Perhaps the fact that my first formal preaching experience was a revival effort partially explains my great love for evangelism today. Just after my ninth birthday, I joined and was baptized in the Zion Baptist Church of Columbia, called by some "Big Zion." The pastor, the late Dr. J. P. Reeder, became my adopted father and, more than any other individual, influenced my development as a preacher.

Since my father and mother separated when I was five years old, my recollection of home is of my mother and the brother and two sisters who were nearest me in age. My mother's religious teachings were more by example than by precept. Prayer before going to bed at night and upon arising was taken for granted. However meager the meal, it was not ever eaten without a "blessing." Caught in the throes of the great depression, I saw my mother struggle to keep her children fed and clothed, and a roof over our heads. We sometimes went days without food and lived through winters with many days and nights of little or no fuel. Often without food or fuel, our home was never without faith! Mama insisted even in the times of greatest emptiness, "the Lord will provide." The songs of her faith were hummed even when worry over rent she was unable to pay drove her to physical illness. While we did not understand the reasons for our poverty, we loved the Lord and were quite certain that he loved us. We were led to feel that any privation which he permitted us to suffer was toward some better purpose in the end. The Bible Reader, which was our substitute for a family Bible, was a book of Bible stories with illustrated pictures. This was THE BOOK in our house!

There was no cataclysmic event to mark either my conversion or my call to preach. There has been no period of my self-awareness when I did not know that I was a preacher. I knew from the earliest knowing of myself that God had chosen me to preach. I have never known any sense of option or alternative with regard to my life's work, nor have I ever wished it to be different. Even so, there is no date to which I can refer as my spiritual birthday. From my beginning, I have believed that Jesus was the Son of God and I have been anxious to tell others of this!

Around my ninth birthday, however, there was a moment which I regard as reaffirmation of my spiritual birth. I sat alone on the porch of our home and prayed that I might be sure of my commission to preach. An awesome awareness of God's presence there so effectively drove away fleeting doubts of my call that never again have they ever crossed my mind. With humble assurance I say with Amos, ". . . the Lord took me . . ." (7:15).

I am thoroughly convinced that the plan and the purpose of God for each human life is precise and that in his providence many convergent lines involving other persons and institutions serve to implement his aim. We can, of course, thwart God's purposes for our lives by our failure to be submissive. At so many points in my life, I have marveled at the way the Lord Jesus has led me to my present opportunities of service.

My family lived in rural Winnsboro County, South Carolina, until shortly before my birth. Had my childhood been spent in that setting, it is certain that my educational opportunities would have been severely limited, for unlike Columbia, there was no local college in Winnsboro. Also, it is unlikely that under those circumstances I would have come into touch with Dr. J. P. Reeder, the father in Christ whose name and memory I bless today.

In my high school, Booker T. Washington in Columbia, there was a Christian teacher who became interested in me and carried me to her home in New York City for the summer. I was then about twelve years old. That development, providentially provided, extended my preaching opportunities throughout the New York City area, where I was widely received and greatly encouraged by many kind pastors and congregations. Their honorariums given in my summers of preaching helped to make the winters more bearable for me and my family. There was even a missionary society in one of the churches, Mt. Sinai of Brooklyn, which took it upon themselves to send me money for milk throughout the next several school years, so great was their concern for my apparent undernourishment. The first car that I owned was bought for me by a godly woman who was a member of one of the churches in that area.

Dr. Reeder took me as his assistant minister, as he had before then taken six other young men, and provided the means for my college education. The total of ten years which I spent with him at Zion, leaving then only against his will, were equal if not superior in value to my formal theological training. In the three pastorates which I have held in the twenty-one years since leaving "Dad" Reeder, many are the times that I have been confronted by pastoral situations for which some solution has come to my mind either from something he said or from the way I saw him handle a similar problem.

When I was only twenty-three years old, I was privileged to preach the introductory, or first, sermon in an Annual Session of the National Baptist Convention of America held at Little Rock, Arkansas. Dr. Reeder was programed to preach since he had entertained the Convention the year before, but he presented me instead. That opportunity to preach led to a widening circle of national friends and preaching engagements throughout the country. The Lord used this means to bring me finally to the attention of both Bethel Institutional Church at Jacksonville, Florida, and St. John Missionary Baptist Church here in Dallas, Texas.

Midway through my pastorate at Bethel, I was called to one of our great pulpits in the city of Chicago. Looking back upon this invitation to serve, which I did not accept, I am now convinced that this was a supreme test of my willingness to surrender the control of my life to God. The Ebenezer pulpit offered more prestige than Bethel, considerably more in the way of financial remuneration, plus the satisfaction of a more challenging pastorate. My resignation to Bethel was withdrawn, however, when I became convinced that God was not transferring me at that time. I have never accepted a pastorate unless I was convinced by certain overt signs that this was, indeed, God's will for me!

The Lord sent me to Dallas through an invitation from the Baptist Ministers' Union of this city to preach in their annual city-wide revival. This was March of 1965, and one year later I took charge as pastor of the St. John Church. I had never before heard of this church, whose eminent minister had just died the previous fall, nor did I even see the church building while I was in Dallas for the revival. As certain as I am that God called me to preach, I am equally certain that he sent me to St. John, to serve as under-shepherd of his flock here! In the five years which have passed so swiftly since my coming to Texas, the Lord has wrought marvelous things through our feeble efforts. For all of these, we give God all of the praise!

The line from a "creek bank church" in my native South Carolina to the St. John pulpit has been long. As a matter of fact, many lines of influence from many individuals and institutions have had to converge to reach this spot in time and place. I am convinced that he who "declareth the end from the beginning" did set my feet in the path leading to this place and that if I am willing to be led, he will lead me onward!

Looming so large in importance in my life that all else is overshadowed by it, the joy of knowing for certain that the Lord calls whom he wills to the gospel ministry and that he has seen fit to choose me has been the subject of my preaching-testimony throughout the years. The following quotes from sermons I have preached earlier illustrate this point.

The Christian Preacher—His Call and Assurance

The experience of the prophets and the reflections of spiritually proven messengers of the new covenant all point toward one unmistakable fact: God deliberately chooses whom he wills to be his spokesman. This should provide no surprise to the reasonable mind, even reasoning from lesser to greater; for what nation would allow a self-appointed ambassador to speak for it? Is not the choice of ambassadors and other representative spokesmen for a nation a matter of the most careful deliberations of the highest councils of that nation? All of this is done to insure that those who speak for a nation shall be responsibly competent to the task. Is there any reasonable ground for surprise or contention to the contrary that God would himself choose carefully those who speak for him and for heaven?

This emphasis is forcibly made in God's call to Jeremiah: "I formed thee . . . I knew thee . . . I sanctified thee . . . I ordained thee, I shall send thee . . . ." (1:5,7). Clearly this is God acting upon Jeremiah; not Jeremiah acting upon God nor Jeremiah acting upon himself. This is no self-choice—this is God choosing.

Since, as in the instance of Jeremiah, the act of choosing by God precedes biological conception and formation, obviously it necessarily predates the preacher-designate's consciouness of being called. That is, God chooses before the preacher-to-be recognizes that he has been chosen. This is nonetheless true whether the recognition of the call comes in early youth or in later maturity, as the dawning consciousness of the call has nothing to do with the act of God's choosing. Any lesser view than this would attribute ridiculously to God the quality of "hindsight," seeing after the event that which might have been more profitably seen before. When one begins to preach, or at least to prepare for preaching, is reflective not of when God called but only of when one hears and answers!

It is to be understood by him that the exercise of choice which results in his calling is reflective only of the sovereign majesty of God and by no means, and in no way, indicates any degree of superiority in the chosen! God chooses whom he will! As in his own wisdom he chose the earth in this solar system to be man's home in all this vastness of space, or as he has made a million other choices independent of any other will or determination than his own, so he has chosen you to preach. He did not choose you because you were the best he had, or because you were the most willing, or because you were the more promising; he chose you to preach because he willed so to do. He is his own determining cause.

Having chosen his messenger, God sends him forth upon heaven's own terms. The preacher is an ambassador to the world, and like ambassadors from lesser powers, the conditions of his functions are carefully prescribed by the Power who sent him forth. The consciousness of being a "sent one" should pervade the minister's being, even as it was indelibly imprinted within the awareness of Jeremiah. After many years, this prophet ponders and reflects upon the great encounter of his life and recalls the words, "I shall send thee . . ." (Jer. 1:7).

The implications of such an awareness are greatly significant, directly to the mental state of the messenger and indirectly to the impression upon the hearers. Knowing that one is sent by God, should for the preacher as for the prophet, remove all appearances of craven deference to worldly power. All too frequently such worldly power is enthroned in control groups within church congregations who would make the preacher's well-being dependent upon their whims and fancies. Truly sent preachers know that pulpits do not belong to pulpit committees; they belong only to God! The appearance of soldiers of the enemies of righteousness are no cause for alarm to the "sent one," when the heavenly hosts are visible hovering nearby. What can a King Ahab do against the King Jehovah? This independent boldness, which the knowledge of being sent gives to the messenger, reflects itself indirectly upon the hearers who develop a greater appreciation for both the messenger and the message. There needs to be something in the bearing and manner of the messenger to make it quite evident that he carries a word of importance. Thus, one of the conditions of heaven set for the functioning of the messenger of the covenant is that he move with fit and becoming dignity and boldness.

Watchmen of Souls

This is always so: responsibility implies accountability. The watchman is chosen and charged with a definite duty—to watch over the city. The selection of a particular person as watchman is evidential of the trust of those who selected him. They believe him both capable and trustworthy. They have no fear that he will fall asleep on the job or wander away from his post of duty. They feel safe in his hands. The imposition of such trust automatically suggests that it must be accounted for. The watchman is not free to do as he pleases, or to not do if he does not wish; he is answerable to those who selected him.

The degree of responsibility is directly proportionate to the value of that for which one is accountable. The watchman over an empty warehouse does not have the same degree of responsibility as a watchman over an exclusive jewelry shop where the on-premise inventory may be valued at millions of dollars. The wall-top watchman has responsibility for a most precious commodity—the souls of men, created by the very breath of God! Beloved by the Eternal, yearned after, much sought, it is not the will of God that a single soul should perish. If one wishes an indication of the value which the eternal God places upon the human soul, he has but to listen to the oft-quoted John 3:16, "For God so loved the world, that he gave his only begotten Son, that whosoever believeth in him should not perish, but have everlasting life."

The responsibility of being such a watchman is staggering! Conceivably, a watchman who, through negligence to duty, loses that for which he is responsible, might be allowed to indemnify the owner and thus be freed of the onus of his failure. But how does one pay for a lost human soul? Since God has set the value of the soul—he gave his Son—what currency can a preacher of the gospel use who has through his dereliction of duty lost even one soul who might have been led to God through Christ? "If the watchman blow not the trumpet . . . if the sword come and take any person

. . . his blood will I require at the watchman's hand. Son of Man, I have sent thee a watchman unto the house of Israel" (Ezek. 33:67). Even with the sure knowledge that one is chosen and sent by God, the temptation in the face of such overwhelming responsibility is to cry out with Moses, "Who am I, that I should go" (Ex. 3:11).

On Having Reason to Stand

In this twentieth century, when the worth and value of preaching is being so brazenly challenged by our secularized culture, we who preach need more than ever to have untarnished "reasons to stand."

"Why am I a preacher?" "Why do I preach?" These are really the self-questions this message would urge you to raise. Do you preach because this "profession" provides a comfortable living and status as a leader in the community? Do you preach because you find yourself unfitted by training and temperament for any other job? Do you preach because you enjoy directing the lives of others or perhaps because your father was a preacher and it was always expected that you would follow in his footsteps? All of these reasons and all other such ones, fall far short of giving you a worthy "reason to stand."

In the simple eloquence of the unpolished language of the herdsman and gatherer of sycamore fruit, Amos, "the Lord took me" is given as a compelling "reason to stand"! Here is the sense of destiny, the unmistakable feeling of being sent by another; but more than that, the sense of being "taken," taken out of self and without regard for selfish desires and purposes! When Amos is lambasted and threatened by Amaziah, the priest of Bethel, for daring to "invade" Israel, coming even to the seat of the government and to the king's court with his prophesy of doom, the reply in defense given by this man of God was simply, "the Lord took me"! Amos assured Amaziah that he would not be at Bethel by his own choosing, and if he had so chosen he would have had no message to proclaim, but he is there because the Lord took him. "I was no prophet," Amos says, "I was no prophet, I was not even the son of a prophet. I was a herdsman and gatherer of sycomore fruit like a thousand others in Judah. Without any special concerns for religion, I was going about my work, tending the flock and gathering the fruit; but the Lord took me, and told me to go and prophesy unto Israel." It was obviously unthinkable to this simple country man that he could continue minding the flock and gathering the fruit after this word from the Lord. These duties must now be left to others; his was a different responsibility, he now had "reason to stand"!

Can any preacher know any more compelling reason for proclaiming the arrival of the King, or dare any preacher go forth with any less compelling reason than "the Lord took me"?

The true preacher of the gospel of Jesus Christ in these days will know his "Amaziahs of Bethel" as certainly as did Amos of Tekoa in the days of Jeroboam of Israel. There will be those vested interests which will challenge his right to speak on certain issues, who will strive by both treats and threats to force his preaching into the comfortably innocuous mold of religiosity. While they will applaud his efforts so long as the voice from the pulpit is liberal with sweet generalities, their anguished cry of "how dare you?" rises quickly when the voice from the pulpit probes the tender spots of their errors and transgressions. They would define for the preacher the proper areas of concern for his sermons, and when their gifts and praise fail to restrain him within these boundaries, they are not averse to threats and pressures.

The response of the preacher who would preach can be no other than that of Amos, "the Lord took me." This takes out of the preacher's hands equally the questions of where he shall preach and what he shall preach. "The Lord, who took me from my way, will set me where he wills. This must be the understanding of the "preaching" preacher. How often the weak preacher rebels in his heart because the place where he stands is not of his choosing! The preacher needs to be reminded that when "the Lord takes a preacher," he sets him to preach in the place of his choosing! Whether in Tekoa of Judah, the prophet's home, or at Bethel at Israel, the king's chapel, the Lord makes the appointment! Whether to a simple people of the fields, or to the sophisticated ones of the royal court, the "reason for standing" is the same: "the Lord took me"!

What the preacher shall say whose reason for standing is that he was taken by the Lord is not of his own choosing, for he is simply to proclaim a message. The word is not his to produce, it is only his to deliver! Obviously then, the messenger cannot tailor his message to fit the desires of his hearers. If he remains faithful to his charge, he can but deliver what the Lord lays upon his heart.

The proclaimer of the King has compelling "reason to stand," because there are dying millions whose very lives, temporally and eternally, depend upon news of the coming of the King! This should be the overriding impression of the preacher who stands in his pulpit and looks out upon the faces of the people in the pews. Most of them are there because they have need; though many of them are incapable of isolating their special need, they are nonetheless needy. Their need is your "reason to stand"! It should hardly be necessary to point out again how utterly you fail them if all you have brought to your pulpit is the lightness of pretty words, or the beauty of logical arguments, or the profundity of your analysis of world affairs. The people in the pews have many needs, but the needs which bring them to church are spiritual needs! Speak to those needs, speak the Word of Life!

The weary and afraid need to be told that the King has come and that there is no longer any reason to fear. The unloved and lonely need to be told that the King has come, and that it was love itself which would not permit him to stay in heaven apart but drove him down to earth to seek and find them. They must be told that loneliness is past, for now they can walk and talk with their Lord, now there is a "tie that binds" them with the blessed fellowship of the redeemed!

The guilt-burdened and despairing must be told that the King has come, and that the black fog of despair is now lifted, for he has taken upon himself the burden of our guilt, and we are made free, indeed, through his grace!

The precious uniqueness of the message given to be proclaimed is perhaps the most important "reason to stand." "How then shall they call on him in whom they have not believed? and how shall they believe in him of whom they have not heard? and how shall they hear without a preacher? and how shall they preach except they be sent?" (Rom. 10:14–15) The man with a sense of destiny comes to the waiting people to speak to them "all the words of this life." The uniqueness of the message colors the personality and dictates the behavior of the messenger. Like the bank messenger who can turn neither to the right nor the left, no matter what the temptation, because of the value of his cargo, the messenger of God must press on; like the diplomatic courier chained to his pouch, because of the importance of his papers, the messenger of God is a "prisoner of the Word"; like the witness circumscribed by firsthand knowledge, the messenger of God can but speak on earth what he hath seen and heard in the heavenly places.

The preacher of the gospel must, like Peter, have unmistakable awareness that there is no place else for the people to go, for Jesus "hast the word of eternal life!" (John 6:68). The daily papers headline the events of the day and seek to influence public opinion, but there is no redemption in their words for they are simply reporters of what has transpired; television takes the people where the news stories are breaking and to talk with the newsmakers, but it can only add to their anxieties and frustrations with the impression of overwhelming events. The study of history may inform man regarding his predecessors, but it cannot redeem, for time is a carrier of both good and evil; science may discover and arrange facts into orderly piles, but it cannot save, for it does not traverse the realms of the spirit nor reach to the areas of ultimate meanings.

"To whom shall we go?" remains as pertinent a question on New York's Time Square as it was on the dusty roads of Palestine, and the conclusion is just as valid, "thou alone hast the word of eternal life!"

This absolute uniqueness of the message, its completely irreplacable value, should fill the preacher of the gospel with a disturbing sense of urgency. Since this word of the arrival of the King is the only word of life available to man, there can be no relaxing, no ease-taking, until every human heart has been given the opportunity to accept the gift of the gospel. It differs but slightly whether the unsaved are the heedless ones in the streets of the cities or the untold ones on the mission fields. "This gospel of the kingdom shall be preached in all the world for a witness unto all nations" (Matt. 24:14). Restless ought be the sleep of the called preacher of the gospel who recognizes that souls are being hurled into eternity every moment and that some have not heard that the King has come.

Should there be fleeting moments when you search for your "reason to stand" as a proclaimer of the gospel of the King, do not linger long in these shadows of half-doubt, for there are compelling reasons for your ministry, sufficiently strong to drive you forward over every obstacle Satan may effect. Resist fiercely any dimming of the sense of destiny, of having been "taken" by the Lord and set in a way of his own choosing. Cling tenaciously to the vision of a waiting people, hungering and thirsting for a "word from the Lord." Keep clear in your mind that only the gospel of Jesus Christ is the word of eternal life, no matter what other "words" may be pressed upon man in this age of many voices!

Maintaining spiritual power for my task is of constant concern to me. The possibility of a powerless ministry drives me often to my knees. The persistent demands for time and attention from other areas of my concern which cut into time needed for devotions is one of the chief frustrations of my ministry. It is exceedingly difficult, sometimes even impossibly difficult, to keep inviolate the times designated for meditation. I have found very early morning hours less vulnerable to the intrusions of these other concerns. To keep rendezvous with the Spirit of the Lord at four o'clock in the morning while the family sleeps and the streets enjoy the brief respite from heavy traffic between late evening pleasure seekers and early morning workers, is for me as refreshing to my spirit as the hours of sleep are to my body. Even more, I enjoy slipping into the sanctuary of the church where I serve in such a still hour, especially on a Saturday night, and standing where I am to stand the next morning to "declare the Word of Life." That beloved place, empty then of worshipers, is often filled for me in such an hour by him whom we worship as I talk with him about the people to whom I must on the morrow talk about him!

In my judgment, no graver danger faces the preacher of the gospel than that in becoming "professionally" competent he should become spiritually impotent! The following is an excerpt from a message which I delivered to preachers entitled "On Lighting the Spark." ". . . your attention has been called to the blacksmith's apprentice who learned how to hold the tongs, how to lift the sledge, how to smite the anvil, and how to blow fire with the bellows. He learned all of this but failed to learn how to light the spark. Alas, this is the sad plight of many who wear clergy garb! They have studied in the seminaries or have had long pulpit experience and are well informed about textual and topical construction, doctrinal and experiential subjects, the arguments pro and con regarding the use of manuscripts, the way the preacher should stand and how he should use his voice. They know all these mechanics, but like the apprentice of the blacksmith, they do not know how to "light the spark"!

It seems obvious to the point of redundancy to say that the preacher who would preach must have a genuinely sincere devotional life. The great danger to this need is the over-development of "professionalism." You know the adage, "the cobbler was so busy making shoes for others that he himself went barefooted."

Some of us go "barefooted" in our devotional lives, so busy are we leading the public worship and calling upon our members to maintain their prayer perspective.

We read our Bibles only in search of a text, never to allow God's Word opportunity to speak to our hearts. The preacher who reads his Bible prayerfully and takes time for "spiritual digestion" does not need to search for a text. As "Dad" Reeder was fond of saying, "texts, one after another, will rush up and say, 'use me.'" So it is; there is more in the Word of God good for the hearts of men than any preacher would be able to preach about in two life times! Make the Bible your stable "spiritual diet." Whatever you may lack in training, whatever you may not know about secular literature, about science, or about art, know your Bible!

The praying preacher is a powerful preacher. If all men ought always to pray, then surely the proclaimer of the King ought to pray! Prayer cleanses and refreshes the soul of the sincere prayer. Prayer gushes wells of spiritual insight, transcending the intelligence of the preacher. Prayer opens doors and melts stubborn hearts. Prayer lifts the man in the pulpit high enough to see heavenly things so that he can come back and share them with the people. Prayer provides the "spiritual vitamins" for the "seven lean years" through which some of us pass, when Satan tries to starve out our faith and trust in him who sent us. Prayer makes keen the spiritual vision to enable you to see the plots and pits before you come to them. The preacher who would preach must be a praying preacher!

Indeed, I feel the need to live a prayerful life, for this clearly seems to be the preacher's path to power.

Jesus Christ has entrusted the leadership of a portion of his flock to my care. Though he charges me with her leadership, he has not even for a single moment relinquished his ownership nor lessened his concern. The flock is his, he is the shepherd; I am but undershepherd of the St. John family.

This knowledge lays upon my heart a terrible burden of responsibility. When priorities make countering claims in the program of the church, I struggle mightily to seek to know the mind of the Lord Jesus. In every such time, I am brought back to that text which he chose for his first sermon in Nazareth, "The Spirit of the Lord is upon me, because he hath anointed me to preach the gospel to the poor; he has sent me to heal the brokenhearted, to preach deliverance to the captives, and recovering of sight to the blind, to set at liberty them that are bruised" (Luke 4:18).

Much less perfectly than he, and depending upon his help for such as I may accomplish; I, also, give myself to this task!

3 BEING BORN ALIVE TO SERVE

Percy A. Carter, Jr.

Behold my servant, whom I uphold; mine elect, in whom my soul delighteth; I have put my spirit upon him." (Isa. 42:1).

"Jesus answered and said unto him, Verily, verily, I say unto thee, Except a man be born again, he cannot see the kingdom of God" (John 3:3).

It is the mission of the church on earth as God's servant and Christ's body to demonstrate creatively and deliberately wherever people are. This demonstration, according to the gospel, consists in the Christian's witness affirming dynamically with conviction that God has the prior claim on our land, our learning, our lives, and our loyalties.

Isaiah 42:1 is no ordinary statement. It is an excluding one. It bars proprietorship by anyone else other than God. The servant of which the prophet Isaiah speaks is the Lord's servant and his alone. "Behold *my* servant, whom *I* uphold; *mine* elect, in whom *my* soul delighteth; *I* have put *my* spirit upon him." Apart from God, this servant does not and cannot exist, for it is God who is doing the upholding, the delighting, and giving the input. It is he who has created and chosen the servant. "*My* servant, my *servant, my servant.*" God chose him. God inspired him. God equipped him. God created him as his instrument. If the servant is ever helpful, it will be because God helps him. If he learns, it will be because he is responding to God's call. If he speaks prophetically *for* God, it will be because he is listening intently *to* God. He will experience victory daily as he obeys God daily. The servant cannot be influential until he is influenced by God. The servant can claim no strength except that which God gives to him. Even the courage of the servant is on loan from God. As the servant's only redeemer, God supplies the courage needed: "O Israel, Fear not: for I have redeemed thee. I have called thee by thy name; thou art mine" (Isa. 43:1).

This emphasis upon the servant as the Lord's servant is consistent throughout the biblical mosaic. The context, the forms, and the writers regarding the servant may change, but the basic biblical truth pertaining to the servant remains the same. There is no communication gap between Isaiah 42:1 and 1 Peter 2:9: "But ye are a chosen generation; a royal priesthood, an holy nation, a peculiar people; that ye should show forth the praises of him who hath called you out of darkness into his marvellous light." The gap that does exist is one of credibility in the church's refusal to do the truth. It is the mission of the church on earth as God's servant and Christ's body to demonstrate creatively and deliberately the gospel truth wherever people are.

According to the gospel, God has the prior claim on our land. "In the beginning God created the heaven and the earth" (Gen. 1:1). The story is told of two little boys who were boasting about the respective merits of their uncles, both of whom had died. The first little boy said: "Wait until you hear this: my uncle left a million dollars when he died." There was a moment of suspenseful silence and then the second little boy replied: "Oh, that's nothing. My uncle left the earth when he died." What we claim here on earth as our material possessions is only ours for a season. We cannot take it with us and we cannot keep it all under our wings. We should live, therefore, knowing that God has made this world in order that we may have a stage on which to carry out our covenant relationship to him and to our fellowman. Speed and media have made the world a neighborhood; but only the love that

Being Born Alive to Serve

God transmits to our lives can make it a brotherhood. We have become confused, secularized, and atomized until we treat people like land and we treat land like people only to stumble over the necessity for the "I—Thou" relationship. Man's careless stewardship of the land is tragically reflected in the stagnating pollution which the land suffers in all forms.

From the world of scientific knowledge, we know now that much of what man considers as new and earthshaking ingenuity has its counterpart in creation and permeates the land. Who said that air conditioning was man's invention? Ever since God made a bee, there have been air conditioning engineers. The temperature outside a bee hive may vary, but the temperature of the brood area inside must be constant if life is to be preserved. As far as we know, the necessary temperature is maintained with no assistance from man. Who said that this is the age of machines and that one day soon machines will outdate organization man? Has anyone designed a machine with a life expectancy of seventy years or more with never shutting off for maintenance and repair? Yet it pumps at least one hundred thousand times per day. Who made the human heart? We commend ourselves on the highly precisioned photographic equipment we are able to produce and adapt for countless situations with supersensitive light meters, instant automatic focus, wide-angle lens, and full-color Polaroid instantaneous reproduction. Yet the human eye has all of these properties and more. Who made it?

We boast about the guidance systems of our aircraft and intercontinental ballistic missiles, but there is an outstanding sea bird known as the Pacific Golden Plover. He breeds in Alaska and winters in Hawaii two thousand miles of ocean away. The parent birds leave for Hawaii first. Several weeks later, the young follow without the benefit of a guide. Who installed their guidance system? The United States Navy uses a sonar system to detect enemy submarines, even as a highway patrolman uses radar to track down speedsters. Identical principles are involved in both cases, and it can be classified under sonar in both cases. Yet, the "blind" bat can avoid obstacles and catch flying insects on any dark night. Who taught him sonar? Someone has said that this is the age of the computer. There is very little that is being built on the land or that is being done to the land or that is deemed beneficial for the land that is not the end product of a computerization process. When one looks at the untold number of trunk-lines that go to make up a world telephone system, it is phenomenal that an American citizen can talk with a relative on the phone "down under" in Asia and the President of the United States can give personal greetings to an astronaut on the moon. Is there any other computer like the human brain that can sort out, store, and act upon the thousands of impulses it receives from the eyes, ears, nose, and both our sensual and tactile networks without having a traffic jam? Who engineered this phenomenal computer? God did it all to perfect our dominion over the works of his hands.

According to the gospel, God has the prior claim on our learning. "If any of you lack wisdom, let him ask of God that giveth to all men liberally" (Jas 1:5). In this day of the new morality and situational ethics, of objectivism and moral relativism, of men getting all they can and canning all they get, we need to take a new lease on learning. Man is not the measure of all things. How else does he know that he is man unless there is someone outside himself by whom he can be measured? Man will not be convinced that he cannot know everything until he meets the one who knows it all. When he has become successful in other outer-space ventures, the universe will still affirm for him that whether on Main Street in Columbus, or Hennepin Avenue in Minneapolis, or the moon over Miami, he is just the tenant and God is the landlord. The concept of his tenantship has much to do with man's concept of himself. The true basis for his identity can only be learned from the truth of God. Around the central core of his tenantship are focused all of his relationships and the learnings therefrom point to man's triumphs and his transgressions. Thus man cries out of

Being Born Alive to Serve

the deep to God, for to know God he must plumb the depths and God is depth because he is truth above and beneath all. Whatever depth our learning has, it is because God has a prior claim on it. He is the source of our knowledge. He is light and in him there is no darkness at all. In him there is light enough to cover all of our darkness and all of our sins.

We can truly make no claim to original knowledge except as we receive knowledge from God. Newton did not really formulate the law of gravitation. Fulton did not really perfect the steam principle. Franklin did not really produce electricity. Edison did not really make the electric bulb, and Carver did not really make cosmetics from the peanut. We speak of them in our vernacular as inventors, geniuses, history makers; but all that they really did was to discover forces at work that were already there—put there by God. So it is in the Christian faith. There are no new theologies or systems of thought that can ever supplant the learning God has already provided for us. At best, there will be many lifetimes of discovering anew the knowledge that even the psalmist felt was too wonderful. "For whatsoever things were written aforetime were written for our learning, that we through patience and comfort of the scriptures might have hope" (Rom. 15:4). The "aforetime" fixes for us God's priority on our learning and places the burden of discovering what is already there on us as his dear followers.

According to the gospel, God has the prior claim on our lives. "For in him we live, and move, and have our being; as certain also of your own poets have said, For we are also his offspring" (Acts 17:28). We do well daily to analyze carefully and sensitively the messages of many voices who stop by merely to tell us that our house is on fire. It is unusual if they remain long enough to help put the fire out and give assistance in repairing or building new houses. Everyday, your life and mine are houses aflame. From problems we seem unable to solve to afflictions for which no medicine has been discovered, we see ourselves aflame. From poverty in the ghetto to battle lines in Vietnam, we see ourselves aflame.

From racism in the heart to violence in the streets to polarization among the people, we are aflame. From varied forms of addiction across our nation to political graft in government and high places, we are ablaze, and the church scattered amidst it all is oft too preoccupied with itself or disenchanted with its constituency to lay bare the need for putting the fire out God's way. From moral breakdown in the home to spiritual "cop out" in the heart, we are burning. This burning is the end result of estrangement from God. Apart from God, we do not live. Our movement is lost and our being is spent.

God recommends in response that we remain attached to him since our very lives depend on it. God has the prior claim on our lives by virtue of his creating us. He made us for himself. Attached to him, we can go anywhere he wants to have us go. Attached to him, there is belonging, purpose, reflection, redemption, and service for all who welcome his pruning. He is the vine and we are the branches. Apart from him we can accomplish nothing. In him are fruit and full joy for life evermore.

According to the gospel, God has the prior claim on our loyalties. "No man can serve two masters: for either he will hate the one, and love the other; or he will hold to the one, and despise the other. Ye cannot serve God and mammon" (Matt. 6:24). Wherever a man's heart is, that is where his loyalties are. Whatever a man serves, that is what he is loyal to and loves. Therefore, no service that he gives to anything can go unheeded or ignored, for every service is an index to his essential loyalty.

For young and old alike today, the word is: "Come alive," "This is the Pepsi generation." Yet some people prefer to limp and loaf. Others go to more trouble to advertise things than to publish the glad tidings of God. How many of us are always going somewhere but never arriving, always receiving but never giving, always believing but never living, always succeding but never striving? It is so easy to become a kind of Mr. and Mrs. Facing-both-ways and actually be looking nowhere. The cheerful optimist said that he

Being Born Alive to Serve

wanted to leave the world better than he found it. The stern moralist replied that if his optimistic friend would just leave the world that it would make a big improvement. Most of us should like to leave the world better than we found it. Our time is lost untangling the confusion of loyalties. We lack the single loyalty of a faith unafraid to leave a lasting impression for loveless moments of despairing phoniness. From such single loyalty, men find a place to stand.

It is noteworthy that a few years ago when a price war on milk occurred in a small western community most of the people involved were reportedly dumping their milk to make a point of protest. But one little lady thought to put the milk she had in an agitator-type washing machine and churn it into butter and sell it. She had some basic loyalties as to what was right and honorable and was willing to stand alone by them. She turned her protest into production. We shall be reading about the milk spillers for sometime to come. It is those persons who have the loyalty and perseverance within to churn milk into butter who add new meaning to life. Each contemporary Christian must reckon with the mandate of God's prior claim on our loyalties: "For do I now persuade men, or God? or do I seek to please men? for if I yet pleased men, I should not be the servant of Christ" (Gal. 1:10).

Only faithful adherence to the truth of God can keep us ever loyal lifting us above our hang-ups. This is very appropriately expressed in the following original poem.

Hang-ups

"And ye shall know the truth, and the truth shall make you free" (John 8:32).

It is so much easier and religious to say:

"I come to you in the name of Jesus Christ." or "Brother, just have faith." For the one who speaks as a Christian

speaks from what is given so oft in such a way as to

nauseate the weak. It is more thoroughly Christian to daily

be a Christian in the power of life in the Spirit.

I am informed that the Christian walk
has a way of covering more purposeful distance than religious talk.
When we are complete in Christ, his presence goes before us and
is transmitted to every life situation.
Sometimes our most complete sentences as Christians
are not a group of religious words grammatically correct and
properly intoned, but a down-to-earth gut-level experience in which
the person seeking becomes the willing object of God's love in Christ,
because God as the chief subject over every moment see fit and can
freely use us as "active verbs" to make salvation practical.

    A warmer hand, a single mind
    Move more fears than a sentence part.
    Even when our lips are used for praying,
    God listens for what the heart is saying.
    What kind of sentence is your life?
        And wherever truth is sacrificed,
        The "hang-ups" soon come home to roost.

Acknowledging God's priority over our lives and all that makes them possible prepares our hearts and minds for sharing the conscience and temper of the servant. The conscience of the servant is the individual realization that you are the Lord's servant. The temper of the servant is to glorify God and declare his praise in the islands of life (see Isa. 42:12). In one of the the well-known Peanuts series of comic strips, Charlie Brown and Lucy were watching Sally as she learned to walk. Charlie asked: "How long do you think it will be before Sally starts to walk?" Lucy replies: "Good grief! What's the hurry? Let her crawl around for a while! Don't rush her! She's got all the time in the world. Once you stand up and start to walk, you are committed for life!" There is error and truth here. The error is that we do not have all the time in the world. The truth is that once we stand up and start, we are committed for life. But who keeps us committed?

In the vernacular of Isaiah 42:3, initially all of us are tall reeds shaken by the winds of life. As smoking flax, at best all we can do is use up our own potential. It is only as God trims us for

Being Born Alive to Serve 55

servanthood that we discover our needs in him. The power, the supply, the assurance we needed has been in our midst all the time, but we lacked the conscience and temper of the servant that God gives us by his grace to discover it. In his strength, we serve for life. Have you seen a plane as it engages in the battle of the runway? When it taxis for the takeoff, there is a battle going on between gravity and aerodynamics. When it takes off, it has won the battle, its weight and cargo, not withstanding. I cannot fully explain it, but I know it works because I have flown. All I do is commit myself to the plane and stay with the program of the plane until the destination is reached. My life is not in the pilot's hands ultimately, but in the hands of of the man who controls the traffic from the towers along the way. Have you ever seen the battle of life's runway for a purposeful life? Between good and evil, light and darkness? With the conscience and temper of the servant, any man can rise above the things of earth when he places his life unreservedly in the hands of God who controls the traffic of life. Without this conscience and temper, there is much lost distance for which we can never compensate in our own strength. God hears the cry of our afflictions. We may despair because God seems to be a long time coming. We may despair, fearing he has reneged on his promise. We do despair, lacking faith and often doubting. But God is faithful. God is gracious. God is dependable. In our despair, we turn to substitutes: our own strength, means and devices—a fad, a craze, a drug, a bug, a trip, a gamble, a smoke, or a mug. The offspring of our fragile and godless substitutes may be free; but they are also uncontrollable, swift, and irresponsible sons of the desert. We have lost so much distance since Adam. Somewhere in Cairo, Cleveland, and Watts, North and South, God's light is still shining because as his you are there.

What then is the divinely ordained mission of the church? As servants of Christ, all must serve. The servant pattern continues. Our functions in the body may be different, our callings may be distinctive and distinguishable, but our oneness in Christ as servants is the same. "But we have this treasure in earthen vessels, that excellency of the power may be of God, and not of us" (2 Cor. 4:7). The lesson of the servant is one of the most difficult lessons for the church to learn and it is also the most important one. Too often, the church has looked at its mission as the world has. The emphasis has been on status rather than function, might rather than right, position rather than propriety, safety rather than suffering, offerings rather than obedience, numbers rather than individuals, works rather than grace, programs rather than power, appearance rather than spirit, preachers rather than people, offices rather than opportunities to serve, and new movements than new creatures. From the New Testament vantage point, the focal point and function of the servant idea is Jesus Christ. "The Son of man also came not to be served but to serve, and to give his life as a ransom for many" (Mark 10:45, RSV). The pattern which Jesus set was one of service. In everything he was supremely the servant of the Lord. No matter how beautiful our churches may be. No matter how well-robed and rehearsed our chancel choirs are. No matter how large the offering or how great the crowd, we must never forget that Jesus Christ did not die in this kind of place. The Scriptures tell us that he suffered outside the gate that he might sanctify the people with his own blood (see Heb. 13:12). Worship is service at its highest when we witness as servants to the lowest.

In John 13:1–17, the New Testament counterpart to the servant idea as found in the Old Testament is very vividly presented. The meaning on the surface of this incident is humility, but the meaning beneath it is even deeper. The deeper meaning is that there is something far more soiling and polluting than the dust of country roads that must be removed if a man is not to be eternally lost, that is the disease-ridden stain of sin. It is this deeper meaning which has meant all the difference in my life and I joyfully give God the praise for it.

One day, while searching through some vital personal papers, I chanced upon a copy of my birth certificate. I had seen it before, but this was the first time that I had taken serious note of some of the wording on it. To think that I had had this piece of paper for twenty years or more and had failed to notice this wording was startling. The names of my parents, the attending physician, and my own were on the certificate. At the time I was examining the information thereon, two words stood out above all the others. These two words were placed above two other phrases related to them. One phrase was in parentheses as follows: (alive or stillborn). A second phrase followed saying: "attested to by the doctor." Above these two phrases were the two words that instantly took on new meaning for me in a manner which I had never contemplated. The two words were: "Born alive!" 9:30 A.M. July 4, A.D. 1929. What a blessed proclamation! What a life-charged truth! What a matchless key! It is the key to all that followed it. For all that followed it could not have happened in my life had I not been "born alive." These precious words immediately brought to mind that oft quoted passage in John 3:3: "Jesus answered and said unto him, Verily, verily, I say unto thee, Except a man be born again, he cannot see the kingdom of God." Of course what Jesus was saying was that physical life, the will of the flesh and the intellectual will while given and important are not in proper perspective until surrendered to and controlled by the will of God. No outward rite or ceremony can accomplish this. The quality of our lives is not transformed by what we do, but by what God does when we truly commit them to him. It is by his mercy that we are transformed and given new life. Daily he stands ready to renew us through the Holy Spirit, our comforter. In reflecting on Christian citizenship, Paul in his letter to his young and trusted helper, Titus, intimates: "For we ourselves also were sometimes foolish, disobedient, deceived, serving divers lusts and pleasures, living in malice and envy, hateful, and hating one another. But after that the kindness and love of God and our Saviour toward men appeared, not by works of righteousness which we have done, but according to his mercy he saved us, by the washing of regeneration, and renewing of the Holy Ghost; Which he shed on us abundantly through Jesus Christ our Saviour" (Titus 3:3–6).

If you will turn to John 3:4, you will notice that Nicodemus was concerned with *how* he could be born again (and for our purposes here, "born alive.") This is the normal human response. We always want to know how things happen. We seem to live in a process-oriented civilization. Much of our talk is on the "how" of anything we may see fit to discuss from *A* to *Z*. How tragic that Nicodemus was so engrossed in the "how" of the new birth that he did not go on to ask "why" at that point also. Even after Jesus gave him an explanation for it, Nicodemus asked again: "How can these things be?" (vs. 9). It was from that point on that Jesus and John spell out the "why" of being born from above (born alive) in that third chapter.

Anyone who does not know Jesus Christ today as Lord and Savior who came to save us from our sins, that person has had a physical birth, but spiritually he is stillborn. Literally he was born dead, "because that which is born of the flesh is flesh" and it cannot know the things of God except by the Spirit of God. Did Paul also not say: "And you hath he quickened [made alive] who were dead in trespasses and sins" (Eph. 2:1).

You can never really understand the how of a particular process until you experience something of the "why" of its existence. Let us examine for a few moments why this new birth which Nicodemus asked about is necessary. In the first place, the man who has not been born of the Spirit of God will be vacillating, unstable, and uncertain. He is a man with one face trying to wear two faces. Therefore, he cannot be depended upon. There is no telling when he will wear which face. This kind of man cannot receive anything from God in the way of faith and humility and essential character until he has been born alive of the Spirit of God (see James 1:5–8). In the second place, the man who has not been born alive can only hope for decay in the end. Death can only lead to decay. It does not have within it any seed that can take it beyond itself. Its very

Being Born Alive to Serve

seed and nature is decay. Therefore, the only alternative to this futile situation is seed that cannot decay. If your life is unholy, the only alternative is a holy life. If you are living in darkness, you must look for light. If you are living in ignorance, you must seek knowledge. If you are living a lie, you must seek the truth. There is no middle ground. If you are stillborn, you need to be made alive. You cannot be both at the same time. He who wants power for life should connect his life to him who is power and life eternal, Jesus Christ. The man who would be "born alive" must be born again, "not of corruptible seed, but of incorruptible, by the word of God, which liveth and abideth for ever" (1 Pet. 1:23). In the third place, since the man who has not been born alive of the Spirit of God is unstable, and since he is in a constant state of decay by virtue of his own sinfulness, all of his joys will be empty and vain until he has entered into true fellowship with the Father and his Son, Jesus Christ. The words which God gives us in the Holy Bible are written and were spoken that our joy might be full (see 1 John 1:3–4). Only the persons who have been born alive of his spirit can know full joy—joy always, joy under all circumstances, joy through all the varied scenes of life, and joy in serving and glorifying God through Jesus Christ.

In the "how" of anything, the main concern is always with process. In the "why" of anything, the main concern is always "motive." Jesus asked on the cross: "My God, My God, Why?" For what reason, to what end, for what purpose, of what origin, of whose design is all this? And in the Sermon on the Mount the emphasis is upon both process and motives. But the burden of the case for the Sermon on the Mount "that of our righteousness exceeding the righteousness of the scribes and Pharisees" rests on motives which are spelled out in specific processes. For example, "Blessed are the pure in heart; for they shall see God" (Matt. 5:7). Thus the Christian's motive is to see God, the process that encourages him to look in this direction is purity of heart. The enabler is God through Jesus Christ. You are not pure in heart because you actually see God, but you desire to see God because you are pure in heart. The motive must precede the process. Look at Matthew 5:9. You do not make peace in order to be called a child of God, but because you are a child of God, you make peace. It is the motive that determines the process, and not the process the motive. These duties that are ours to perform as Christians, as servants, are not performed to make us so, but because we have been born alive, we do them. We act in a peculiar way because we have been peculiarly born again and alive!

Finally there is a very prophetic sequel to this question of "how" that Nicodemus raised. And it occurs in a later experience of Nicodemus. In John 19:39, we are told that "There came also Nicodemus, which at the first came to Jesus by night, and brought a mixture of myrrh and aloes, about a hundred pound weight." From this experience, we learn why many people are never born alive of the Spirit of God. We receive an insight relating to the "how-why" tension in our lives. Here Nicodemus brought gifts to anoint the body of Jesus. Just a bit earlier, Nicodemus had denied having any connection with Jesus as a Pharisee. When he could have spoken a word in testimony of Christ, he would not. He felt satisfied to ask a safe question rather than give a true answer. He chose the safety of his own house above the convictions and crosses of a true believer in Jesus Christ. Nicodemus apparently had not seriously considered the "why" of being born alive. He was so engrossed in the "how" that he could not even pause to consider the "why." And so he brought gifts to anoint the body of Jesus. This was a very fitting act in deed, but the question of "why" was still an alien to him. And so it is with us as human beings. We are content to raise the question of "how," to ask the safe questions regarding the Son of God (the "how" questions) rather than claim him as our Lord. We are satisfied to religiously bring gifts to anoint his body often not knowing that our gifts to him will not save us. The things we do in his name cannot deliver us from the snares of sin. Only the sacrifice of ourselves born alive of his Spirit because

Being Born Alive to Serve

he first loved us can give us the grip on life we need. You will begin to realize anew why you must be born again. God has fixed it so that the tension of "how and why" of "prices and motive," "of the desire to do good and the will to do it," is resolved in what he has already done and our being quickened by his Spirit through faith in him. Yes, he "so loved the world that he gave his only begotten Son, that whosoever believeth in him should not perish, but have everlasting life." O how wondrous; yet how unworthy am I; Christ died that I might be born alive to serve. If we have been born alive, his presence will attest to it even as some doctor attested to the status of your birth. Of course, the miracle is, God can change your status from "stillborn" to "alive" when you wholly receive Christ as Lord of your life today—right now.

Above all things as a Christian, as a pastor, as a son, as a husband, as a father, and most of all as a servant, this is what Jesus means to me: Being born alive to serve. People come to the church weak and often heavy-laden. Too oft we tell them to strive and struggle only to have them arouse the muddy sediment of sin from the puddle in which they find themselves. Too often, all we do is put an antiseptic in the water of our own choosing and merely exchange one form of impurity and pollution for another. Only the blood of Jesus Christ cleanses us from all our sins. We tell them to get hold of themselves, to confine their problems to one segment or corner of their lives. But the mud has already gone to work. Nothing seems to bring release. There is only one way out. Tell them to turn away from the dirt and mud to the light. Let them see that light in you—the light of Jesus Christ—the light of the world. He arose with power to keep that light shining for other sheep whom he would bring into the fold.

I know a man who saw that light one day. The man was lame. He was laid at the gate called Beautiful. He was left alone until Peter and John came. He was looked on. He was loved. He was lifted up. He leaped from infirmity to life, from a groundling to a witness, from a beautiful gate to redeeming grace, from a beggar to a child of God. Thank God for this living parable of service. The generation of people we serve is a lame generation. They lie daily at the gate of the Temple asking alms of Christians who enter. Can they look on us? Do we love them enough to lift them in the name of Jesus Christ? His power alone will cause them to leap, to stand, to walk, to enter the Temple praising God.

If the power of Jesus Christ as the Servant of God could pull the nails out of every Christian's cross and enable us to know him in the power of his resurrection, then that same power can make any man who repents of his sins and believes, a servant born alive to serve.

> A charge to keep I have,
> A God to glorify
> Who gave His son my soul to save,
> And fit it for the sky.
>
> To serve the present age,
> My calling to fulfil
> O may it all my powers engage
> To do my Master's will.
>
> Arm me with jealous care,
> As in thy sight to live;
> And O Thy servant, Lord, prepare
> A strict account to give.
>
> Help me to watch and pray,
> And on thyself rely.
> By faith assured I will obey
> For I shall never die.

4 WHAT JESUS MEANS TO ME

Nelson H. Smith, Jr.

It has been well stated that there is not only a gospel according to Matthew, Mark, Luke, and John, but a gospel according to each individual who has had a personal encounter with Jesus Christ and from this personal knowledge of the Lord Jesus comes a willing testimony of his redeeming grace.

The apostle Paul, in writing his first letter to the Thessalonians, makes a statement that substantiates the foregoing words: "So being affectionately desirous of you, we were willing to have imparted unto you, not the gospel of God only, but also our own souls, because you were dear to us" (1 Thess. 2:8).

In spite of the joy and gladness that fill the heart of every follower of Jesus and the willingness of testifying to everyone one meets, how is it possible to tell with the clarity I desire and the power that it deserves what Jesus means to me? Just how can anyone really express his innermost feelings, either with crippled language or eloquence or words?

Perhaps the best approach is to give a brief history of my life, beginning in the home of Christian parents, with a father who was a pastor of several rural churches and a mother deeply committed to the Christian faith.

One of the greatest blessings of my life was to have been born black, a male, and in the South. I doubt if I could have said this ten years ago, but I have had experiences where Jesus has revealed himself in such a marvelous and miraculous way. Perhaps this reliance on him would have been by-passed, had my circumstances been different. The strength I needed was provided, and out of many events, real or imaginative, his example has given an anchor for my life. Jesus Christ has always been the hope of the suffering masses. His ministry was always to those who existed in misery.

I was born the third child and first son of Reverend and Mrs. N. H. Smith, Sr. A small, sawmill town, Brewton, Alabama, is the place of my birth. My father was a pastor and teacher-principal. My mother taught also during these early years.

My Encounter with Jesus

Honesty compels me to give the setting as it actually happened relative to my conversion experience. To do otherwise would distort the facts without doing justice to my black experience.

With my father pastoring a church, being principal of a church-related school, my world was primarily the church. This triggered in me a desire for the spiritual. I wanted more than anything else a personal encounter with Jesus of Nazareth that I heard so much talk about.

The gospel I heard was presented to me in the black preaching idiom. The preacher would show all of us who sat on the "mourners bench" as it was called, what would happen to "sinners in the hands of an angry God." Perhaps some of us came to Jesus out of fear. Naturally, the thoughts of eternal punishment in hell or eternal life with God in heaven had great influence on our decision.

Yet, the more I think of it, my father and mother taught me that accepting Jesus as my Savior must be a voluntary act on my part. My yes to him would mean nothing without the choice also of being able to say no. They reminded me often that Jesus will not override one's will. He is always knocking, pleading, desiring to enter my life, but in faith I would have to open the door of my heart and invite him in.

The kind of preaching I heard often caused sleep to bypass me, and appetite was lost. This is no picked-up expression, it happened to me. Where or when the practices started, I do not know. But they formed the events surrounding my conversion experiences.

I can remember so vividly that revival meeting the last week in September, 1939. The visiting revivalist that year was Reverend E. B. Tyson, pastor of the Bethel Baptist Church, Montgomery, Alabama. He preached with "soul" and possessed a strong persuasive technique, urging me to accept Jesus. He made clear that I was to accept what God had done for me through his Son, Jesus Christ on the cross. He never made that oft repeated phrase, "give me your hand, and give God your heart." He offered me the plan of salvation from Romans, Chapter 10.

He cautioned me that salvation is impossible without faith. As he pleaded with me, some mysterious force held me back. Then he turned and used the traditional "whoop" with a ring of the coming judgment.

I did not have any traditional prayers to pray, but my state of not knowing Christ drove me to tears. I can remember it so well. Monday and Tuesday, my faith was too weak for me to step forward. Then came Wednesday afternoon. I was dressed in a suit and shoes ordered from Spiegel's catalog, the only suit I would get until the next revival or commencement exercises. The whole outfit cost less than six dollars.

I was told to get on my knees as the custom was. Members of the Deacon's Board and Missionary Workers came and touched me on my head saying; "Trust him son." "Don't doubt him." "He will save you right now." Finally, the prayer was over, and I got up from my knees, standing there facing the minister. This overall concern for my salvation from the whole church shook me visibly. Suddenly, I walked forward and sat down, giving the minister my hand. Screams were heard throughout the sanctuary.

You who read this account of my encounter with Jesus may see this as something strange, vague, unthinkable or even totally incomprehensible. But it happened to me. It is as clear now as if it happened yesterday. I was saved that day, and I am being saved, and I shall be saved. A nine-year-old black boy had a personal, real encounter with Jesus Christ. It was the greatest moment of my life. This is true of any individual who accepts Jesus Christ as his personal Savior. There is a new creation for anyone who is in Christ.

I felt a kinship to the heavenly, a kind of mysterious transformation had taken place. I felt a sense of belonging not before known. There is a reality in the event, not just some child's act without significance and being knowledgeable of my action. It was real! Very real!

My Early Religious Training

My early religious training came primarily from three sources, home, church, and church-related schools.

In addition to my father being pastor, principal, teacher, he was equally known as a disciplinarian. He meant what he said when he said it, although he was a kind, compassionate man.

My mother was a soft-speaking person. Yet, one could easily discover the firmness in that soft voice. Her general attitude and temperament made her one of those noble souls not ever forgotten by anyone who knew her.

In all three institutions where I received my early training, Jesus Christ was the central subject. Some of my teachings were vague and to me unrealistic, but to question was out of the question.

It was mandatory in our home for daily Bible reading. As soon as each child learned to read, simple portions of Scripture was selected for our daily meditation. Even around the breakfast table on Sunday morning, in addition to prayer, we sang a song and recited a Scripture passage that we had committed to memory. This kind of practice created within me a deeper interest in spiritual things.

There were many "don't's" taught in our home. No card playing, no dancing, no listening to "worldly music," no shooting marbles or playing ball on Sunday. Christmas was a "holy" day, not a holiday, so no shooting fire crackers.

Discipline was an accomplished fact in our home. Therefore, who is going to argue? Yet, this discipline was in love. As the Bible says, "Ye fathers, provoke not your children to wrath: but bring them up in the nurture and admonition of the Lord" (Eph. 6:4).

When I knew myself, attending worship was already established. Each Sunday, we made our way to Sunday School. With my father having more than one church, on those Sundays he was away, there were other activities.

With keen reflection, there is only one experience in my early religious exposure that I did not enjoy, and that was attending the Sunbeam Band meeting. This group was made up of small children, and following Sunday School on "off" Sundays, we would meet. The other boys my age appeared to have had a choice, I did not. It was imperative that I attend. So, I made the best of it, even though I cannot remember anything happening that made any kind of impression.

The Vacation Bible School, meeting two weeks each summer, was always an anxiously anticipated event.

Those who conducted this program made Christ "live" for us. There was a kind of understanding received that I missed in many other church activities. It was during Vacation Bible School where I learned the story of the prodigal son. Someone had written a play, "The Prodigal Son." This was my first experience where *dramatics* were used in understanding Bible stories. I was given the part of the prodigal son. We presented the play in such a way that it became the talk of the community. The white Methodist church requested that we present it there. This was my first experience of being inside a white church.

Because of this experience, I began to wonder about the barriers between black and white. Even though my parents never talked to me about there being a "special" place for me, or that I was to "behave" a certain way around white people, I was led along a certain "carved" path.

We were religiously taught to love and respect everyone. Never can I recall a distinction being made in our respect for people. However, living in a small community, one gets to know most people, black and white. I reflected on the differences. All of the advantages were in their favor and so few in ours.

My Christianity had taught me that God so loved the world. That people who accepted Christ had one badge of identification, and that was love for one another. Does not God see us all equally as his children? This kind of discovery can be and has been a great shock to black people for nearly four hundred years. However, when one looks at the historical background of black people being introduced to Christianity by white evangelicals, one can understand that much of the Christianity taught in the Western world does not coincide with what the New Testament teaches. Christianity as practiced in the Western world leaves out the universality of the gospel and the inclusiveness of all men in an integrated, loving fellowship.

Questions came to my mind: Is Christianity as taught me some kind of pacification, leading me into a state of satisfaction, yet offering no real solution to the human dilemma? Is this some kind of propaganda that is taught to help the black man survive?

At this early age, however, thoughts as deep as these were temporary flashes of something to come later on.

My Early Church Life

My early church life was traditionally routine. Church attendance was done with trip-hammer regularity. Even though routine, it formed almost my total world. I was free to be involved in church life always. Because of this, the church is serious business with me. I don't enjoy being around anyone who takes it lightly, in spite of the failures and irrelevance of many church programs and practices.

The church purchased the house in which I was born. The

church furnished the money, such as it was, for all my necessities in childhood, youth and adult life.

It was in the church where my first friendships were formed. It was in church where the scales of unbelief fell from my eyes and my "feet shod with the preparation of the gospel of peace." It was in the church where great questions were raised, and life became meaningful and purposeful to me. The church was not only a religious institution for me, but a social center of the black community. It still is. I am always disturbed when any black person speaks unkindly about the church. It has done more for blacks than any other institution we have known.

There is always an advantage in attending church-related schools. They offer a different kind of education. In fact, the church gave birth to education. And in many instances, there is found a different kind of instructor, having keen perception, and a far deeper commitment to their task.

The first school I attended was the Bethlehem Industrial Academy, a church-related school, founded by the Colored Bethlehem Association. Classroom work was fascinating, but chapel assembly, which was a daily practice, was the event I looked forward to.

A different teacher would be in charge each week, and on Fridays, the principal, Professor H. J. Lamar, taught the Sunday School lesson for the following Sunday.

The theological bent from my church and school was basically fundamentalism. But from time to time certain insights came through to me in a very convincing way. Yet, there was something missing, a kind of inconsistency kept creeping up. Explanations were often vague, but my curiosity deepened.

Many times following the chapel period, the Sunday School lesson became the topic of discussion in the next class period. Teachers were eager to hear our comments, hoping that these lessons would give us a firm religious foundation. Not only were spelling, mathematics, science, history, and literature necessary, but each student needed to find purpose and meaning for his life. And only Jesus Christ gives purpose and meaning to life. His teachings show that man needs the will to be and God gives him the power to become. The aimlessness seen in so many individuals comes from the fact that life for them has no purpose, aside from "eating, drinking, and being merry." They exist because they breathe, and breathing becomes their chief concern. Life should be viewed as a precious gift from God, and spent in useful service. A line from a creed I learned in school has been a kind of motto for me throughout my involved life: "I believe that the life of service is the life that counts; that happiness endures to mankind when it comes from having helped lift the burdens of others."

When I think of my conversion experience, my early religious training, the efforts put forth in developing a devotional life, I will never agree with those who say that Christianity is the white man's religion, being fed to black people so that they will quietly and passively accept a negative status in this world. However, I will admit it is a difficult task for a black pastor to make the gospel meaningful to black people who have never tasted any spoils of victory or known a calm and peaceful existence.

The very heart of Christianity is that men are to love one another. And I can say truthfully that whatever misery, denial of my rights, and all other hostilities experienced as a black man, I have no hate, bitterness, or ill-will toward anyone.

Tell me where else in the world can one find that kind of strength save in his Lord Jesus Christ? Among everything else that he means to me, he is my help and my high tower in a world smeltering with injustice and inequities. Among everything else he means to me, he is my life, my joy and my salvation.

My Call to the Ministry

The call to the Christian ministry and my commitment to the black struggle are all tied together in the idea of my self awareness. My encounter with Jesus Christ at this point is similar to that of the prophet Jeremiah. Here is Jeremiah, sitting on the stage of life with a "seething pot" on one side and "an almond tree" on the other side. As he ponders his dilemma, a voice speaks to him, "What seest thou?" Jeremiah, the weeping prophet, is caught between doom and duty. Here is just a boy in the middle of despair and hope, justice and injustice, war and peace. Jeremiah knew where the word came from. No illusions cluttered his judgment; the word was clear. "Before I formed thee in the belly I knew thee; and before thou camest forth out of the womb I sanctified thee, and I ordained thee a prophet unto the nations. Then said I, Ah, Lord God! behold, I cannot speak: for I am a child. But the Lord said unto me, Say not, I am a child: for thou shalt go to all that I shall send thee, and whatsoever I command thee thou shalt speak. Be not afraid of their faces: for I am with thee to deliver thee, saith the Lord. Then the Lord put forth his hand, and touched my mouth. And the Lord said unto me, Behold, I have put my words in thy mouth. See, I have this day set thee over the nations and over the kingdoms, to root out, and to pull down, and to destroy, and to throw down, to build, and to plant. Moreover the words of the Lord came unto me, saying, Jeremiah, what seest thou? And I said, I see a rod of an almond tree. Then said the Lord unto me, Thou hast well seen: for I will hasten my word to perform it. And the word of the Lord came unto me the second time, saying, What seest thou? And I said, I see a seething pot; and the face there of is toward the north" (Jer. 1:5-13).

As a seventeen-year-old boy, black, a member of the community of the hurt, I found myself on the stage of life. Sitting there between hurt and healing. On one side of me was deprivation, and on the other side was a people, dehumanized, disfranchised, and fragmented. But the word came clearer and clearer. No argument was given, I only felt a total sense of inadequacy. But possibly, there is where God's messenger is always caught, between the "seething pot" and "an almond tree." He is always situated between a needy people and a sufficient God. This was my dilemma.

At this point, reflections on my encounter with Jesus Christ assured me of his abiding presence. I thought of him not as a figure in history but a present help and constant friend.

During the six years I spent at Selma University, I heard a sermon by Dr. Ralph Mark Gilbert that caused a turning point in my thought pattern. His presentation so penetrated my mind and heart that I had to reevaluate some concepts I had of preaching the gospel, the mission of the church, and man's purpose in the world.

From this point of thrust, I have been searching for greater realities of the Christian faith and the kind of relevance and theological thinking that met people where they were.

My experience as a black pastor, working with people who have been hurt, bruised, misused, abused, beat up, bombed out, and shot up, has given me a reliance on Jesus Christ that no other experience could have given me. He is my Lord and Master, totally alive in my experiences, constantly there, guiding, challenging, and protecting my life into meaningful channels of activity.

There is a concept of Jesus Christ and his church based primarily on the black experience. The status of the black man in the United States has always been one of frustration, segregation, and discrimination. Only Jesus Christ, his example and teachings could have given the black man hope and the unction to function.

My involvement in Christian social action took on new dimensions when I came to Birmingham, Alabama, as pastor of the New Pilgrim Baptist Church. This church accepted a new kind of ministry. The old method of being committed to the mission of the church two hours on Sundays has caused disenchantment as well as dismay in the minds of adults and the youth. The church has for too long turned its ministry within, rather than without. After worship on Sunday morning, there is no involvement during the rest of the week. Man's problems are daily problems.

The late Dr. Vernon Johns said often that whatever an individual needs to live a normal life was a spiritual matter. These included food, clothing, shelter, consequently, jobs.

Whatever it is that keeps a person from being fully human, living up to all his potentials, should be eradicated from society, with the church taking the lead. Injustice has hindered, from my own knowledge, most minorities in this land. Segregation and discrimination have crippled millions. The denial of quality education has maimed millions. The barriers to economic stability have many in the state of despondency.

These things and others negate the efforts of people of a darker hue to find themselves a place in the sunshine of God's blessings. The church of Jesus Christ must initiate programs and delete practices that hinder and hurt any of God's children.

The New Pilgrim Baptist Church has instituted several programs to help people, black and white. In spite of most members in black churches receiving low wages from whites, they have shared their meager earnings for worthwhile programs. Our church operates a Day Care Center, a Mobile Service for Human Development, a Federal Credit Union, a Strong Benevolent Program, and supports vigorously organizations working for social improvement.

Dr. Martin Luther King, Jr., the Moses of the twentieth century, had the greatest impact on my life, second only to Jesus, as being involved in the world where people are. Many members of New Pilgrim Church and myself have gone to jail to secure rights for the oppressed. The church must go where men and women have been thrown on the junk piles of society and pick them up, straighten them up, as well as cheer them up.

The life of Jesus gives me a sense of identification. When I reflect on where he was born, how he was "despised" and "rejected," I can identify with him. I can pray for my enemies as he did. I can bless from my bleeding and serve joyously in my suffering. This is one of the greatest things he can mean to anyone. As one gathers love for the oppressor, and commits himself to work for reconciliation, the presence and power of Jesus are gloriously felt. He means to me that in following his example, to do the will of the Father, a heavenly sense of fulfilment comes into my life, with a knowledge that immortality has been realized when in giving my life, I will receive life everlasting.

5 WHAT JESUS CHRIST MEANS TO ME
Charles E. Boddie

Jesus Christ, Superstar,
Are you what they say you are?

The burden of the testimony set forth here is to be based upon personal rather than hearsay aetiology. The treatment will in no way be influenced by images projected by wit or by quip from the way-out catalysts, the "Johnny come latelys" who may be fascinated by the immediacy of "instant redemption" which the Jesus Movement seems to have spawned with a speed exceeding that of light, counteracting that deadly "speed" which the hard stuff generates.

His life at once touches mine at four points. He means all to me as Redemptor, Preemptor, Precursor, and Exemplar. To tell just exactly how that man from the obscure village of Nazareth entered into my life with such force as to become for me "life's greatest astonishment" taxes all powers of expression. In spite of the poverty of language, written or vocalized, we strike out with temerity, pleading for your prayers.

Over my head in the office where I labor hangs a picture of Jesus, a spin-off from the aesthetic mind of the deaf albeit artistic Signe Larsen, copyrighted in 1933. When my day starts with the usual private devotion, my eyes meet the eyes of Jesus as he holds his sturdy, agrarian face as steadfast as it must have been when head-ing toward the Jerusalem Holy City. Beneath the rugged earthy countenance are inscribed the oft repeated phrase in the prayer he taught his disciples: "Thy kingdom come." The challenge that is mine in this prayer experience, by the picture's very hanging presence, is to cogitate over the reminder from his words—and the penetrating gaze from the eyes of that "Am Haretz"—that the kingdom cannot break into our money-centered, dehumanizing world culture unless it begins with me. It tells me that "Lord, Send a Revival," and let it begin in me is more than a threadbare children's prayer meeting ditty. It is a specific appeal to my sense of loyalty to the highest and best that I know, that it may have direct bearing on assisting in the dynamiting of the darkness which bedevils our melancholy days. That face takes all of the "who me?" out of his command to carry out his commission, prompting categorical acceptance of my involvement in the immediate responsibility that is mine to move out "to the work" of helping to bring in his kingdom.

Jesus Christ as Redemptor

The Bible passage reads: "You shall call his name Jesus, for he will save his people from their sins." Just how that name relates to that mission is not too clear. It would seem a well nigh insuperable task to achieve success in such a colossal venture, whatever empowerment could be supplied by whatever name. To save from one's sin (depravity), it seems, is far more difficult than to save from one's sins (naughtinesses). Jesus seems destined by virtue of a name to "save to the uttermost." My fascination for him as touching the whole matter stems from his concern for me as being so deep and wide that he willed to redeem me in that particular Calvary fashion, from the consequence of my crimes, depravities, and unworthy actions; in short, my sin. From the many to the one, he chooses to seek me out for a great salvation, seeking to know with his Father the actual number count of the very hairs upon my head. I simply cannot get over this overwhelming episode of outpouring particularity. I, too, can scarce take it in.

I recognize the biblical fact that Jesus came preaching, teaching, and healing. But to contemplate on the fact, as above expressed, that his real reason for coming was to save me from my sin, devastates. And to think that the only way it could be done was the way it was done, well nigh ruins me. To explain, the poverty of language would fail anyone, but in spite of my paralysis induced by the great wonder of it all, shall we plod on.

In a poll to determine the most important events which gave real significance to human worth, these are listed in the order of rank: the issuing of the Magna Carta at Runnymede, the conversion of Constantine, the invention of the wheel, the discovery of fire, the writing of the Declaration of Independence, the composing of the Bill of Rights, the issuing of the Emancipation Proclamation, and the Battle of Waterloo. Had the opportunity been given me to submit a choice, the crucifixion of Jesus Christ, which tied for eighth place with Waterloo, would have headed the list. No wonder that today's humanity is on the brink of meeting its Waterloo! Today's most fruitful mission field is America's suburbia. John Updike's *Couples* proves how badly the many-forked rake of missionary outreach is needed to scrape over the immoral ground found behind the crabgrass curtain. This swinging generation may yet do us in as it out-Sodoms both Babylon and Gomorrah.

I suppose we are rescued in dealing with the fact as ponderous as the redemption experience as touching the Calvary event by simplifying everything when attempting abortively to explain it. The sheer simplicity of one of Christendom's most famous song types, "What a Friend We Have in Jesus," merely tickles the ridges of the colossal kernel truth of the redemption. And yet, in the face of it, what else can one do but take advantage of the "privilege to carry everything to God in prayer," and make use of the simple song prayer of gratitude:

> Thank you Lord, for saving my soul;
> Thank you Lord, for making me whole,
> Thank you Lord, for giving to me
> Thy great salvation, so rich and free.

Admittedly all of this likens itself to the frustrated efforts of the little boy passenger visiting Niagara Falls on the "Maid of the Mist," standing on its bow trying blandly and blindly to scare up some verisimilitude from his own juvenile vitals by shooting the spurting contents of a water pistol at the mighty cataract. In the face of such a bewildering happening of atonement, what else can one do but babble out inane banalities? Before the awful fact that the Redemptor behaved as he did upon that cross for me, I am reduced to utter impotence and sheer silence.

Wherein, then, come my shouts of "Hallelujah!"? What is it that spiritually turns me on? Why, the glorious admitting of the salvation act as a fact for me, if I believe. This is what W. W. Boone, the evangelist who converted me, said; and the five-year-old lad had no better sense than to believe him. The sheer simplicity of it frightened even then and still scares off the sophisticates. When I recognized that here was an event that defied "figuring out," I found my peace. "Only believe, and thou shalt see, that Christ is all in all to thee." Seeing is not believing, believing is seeing.

My reward? Through all of the trials and tribulations undergone, as trouble has often sought to batter me down, and loads were carried, and thorny pathways trod, he has treated me so good that there actually have been times that I was lead to almost believe that I was the only child that he owned. He did not lift the burden, but supplied strength to carry it. He did not smooth out the path, but directed my feet as I traversed the thorny way. Ask, please, for no explanation. The best I can do at the moment is to rely upon Harry Webb Farrington to attest to my positive conviction as touching the validity of all of this when he wrote:

> I know not how that Bethlehem's Babe
>   Could in the God head be;
> I only know the Manger Child
>   Has brought God's life to me.
>
> I know not how that Calvary's Cross
>   A world from sin could free;
> I only know its matchless love
>   Has brought God's love to me.
>
> I know not how that Joseph's tomb
>   Could solve death's mystery;
> I only know a living Christ,
>   Our immortality.

On a local television program I was asked the meaning of the black experience. I immediately replied: "The third verse of the number one hit song of the day:

> Through many dangers, toils, and snares
>   I have already come;
> 'Tis grace hath brought me safe thus far,
>   And grace will lead me home.

My feeble attempts to match the extravagance of Calvary have proven futile so far; but whatever it is that makes me feel that in spite of my unworthiness and frustration, I belong, is to me truly "amazin.' "

For so fully meeting my need, and adequately endowing me with the capacity to baptise it into a satisfaction for my deepest craving, he places me in his eternal debt. Whatever else I may or may not do, my belief in him, somehow triggering a like belief on his part in me, in the light of such love and grace from my Redeemer to me vouchsafed, all of this demands "my soul, my life, my all."

Jesus Christ as Preemptor

Calvary was the guarantor for the real victor in that encounter with the forces of sin presided over by Satan. It had seemed that the race for the preemptor's rightful station had been won by the evil one by Adam's error; but to believe that is to err. The real winner and still champion is as clear as the Easter sunburst. By his resurrection, Jesus Christ by that act seized, before anyone else did or could, the ownership of eternal life, eternal verity, eternality in all of its forms, to be dispensed thereafter only according to his terms, by him, and him alone. Should we or anybody else settle in upon his domain as squatters, our status is changed from intruding, spurious possessors, to rightful owners, no longer strangers but welcomed citizens. And he is the one that makes this possible. The Pauline treatment of our interloper status which changes us from bastards to sons is true only because he handled the complicated matter on the cross. And here again the act of simple belief, so mandatory in laying ahold of eternal verity bewilders, but believe it we must. "Blind unbelief is sure to err," says Isaac Watts. But we are here dealing with clear-sighted belief; a certitude which, if not just that, would have caused to occur a long time ago a breakdown in the equilibrium of spiritual forces, and chaos long since would have reduced all to a rubble of absolute nonsensical nothingness. It took the five-year-old boy a few more years to latch on to this truth; but, once having allowed a little light to shine through, refracted against the prism of childlike belief far from being blind, there came the opening up of the heavenly sluices of light which made him more fully aware of the abundant riches of his Lord, and then thus became his slave. Try as one might, he is unable to improve upon the way the great apostle phrased it: "By whose poverty we have become rich."

In so conducting himself, the Preemptor becomes at the same time something of a divine interloper. Not that he forces his way into one's life, but like some holy gadfly, appears on some Emmaeus Road and makes himself so indispensible by his proffer of redemptive helpfulness that he needs not a begging on the part of the renewed spirits for entrance into the heart's home. Upon our first move suggesting a hint of importunity and constraint, even though the night is far spent, he accepts the invitation and comes in to sup. There is no other way to explain the perfect character of that third man on that seven-mile stretch of road, who not only revived the flagging spirits of Cleopas and his companion, but before he was through, also had turned the two candidates for suicide into flaming evangelists. Although we, too, must "constrain him" because of his innate tendency "to go further," he surely responds to my invitation and yours to come in for supper. He had a similar meal at the home of Zacchaeus, but not until, in the importunate act of a shin-barking tree climb to better see him, did the invitation find acceptance by all parties concerned. You simply have to "constrain him." After that comes the ecstasy and the deliverance.

Nicodemus, seeking a solution to a philosophic problem, coming by night for an interview, found in that very act of importunity a ready response, and the two inquirers probably burned the midnight oil over the (to me) innocuous question of how a man can be born twice. Never mind how innocuous; he responds to our every need and wish to encounter him if in good faith we constrain him however insignificant the need might seem to others to be.

My "Father shall supply your every need, according to his riches in glory," if one constrains him.

Four men carried a cripple on a litter to the feet of the Healer. In this act of Christian teamwork, each was vindicated for taking his single place at the four corners of the bedstead. Their constraint required the moving with their burden through crowds, and the dismantling of a neighbor's roof. I say, each found his vindication when the Master Healer was heard to say: "Thy sins be forgiven thee" and because of the faithful constraint of these who carried you hither, "rise up and walk." What a reward for teamwork; what a vindication for constraint; what a triumph for faith! "There's a stranger at the door. Let him in!"

By his Calvary experience Jesus Christ possesses truth's domain as both preemptor and interloper; meddles in my affairs and yours, even as he waits us out to invoke his aid to help us straighten them out.

> Our lives through various scenes are drawn,
> And vexed with trifling cares,
> While Thine eternal thought moves on,
> Thine undisturbed affairs.

I cannot disturb his affairs; but, in helpfully meddling in mine as preemptor-interloper, so becomes my prophet, my priest, and my king.

In concluding one of his letters, the apostle uses a benediction, which, for all of its ungrammatical character, is clear in the light of all of this: And now unto him who is able to do exceedingly abundantly more than we are able to ask or think, to the only wise God our Father, be glory in the church, and throughout all generations now, henceforth and forever. Thank God for the invasion in my life of the divine intruder, who awakens my slumbering conscience in the preempting, bothersome, but saving presence of Jesus Christ! Without such, how could I attain unto a fitness to receive him into my heart's home?

Jesus Christ as Precursor

The overwhelming experience of being the recipient of all good as a result of my acceptance of his free grace, is the basis of my assurance that because he has so blessed me here that he will remember me there. Here is the intercessor, assured by the power which Calvary and the resurrection clothed upon him, not only interceding, but running ahead of me as an holy harbinger heralding the sure entrance of my soul into eternal rest. Here is the Christ, as it were, in the guise of the holy roadrunner who settles down only when he has, like Francis Thompson's "Hound of Heaven" successfully tracked me down. He wants to save me more than I want to be saved. His boundless love is the kind that rests not until his restless one finds his rest in him. I believe in this relentless "sniffer outer," the great forgiver; the Father, who stands on tiptoe scanning the horizon for the hoped-for return of his prodigal son; the salvation of the thief whose tardy penitence is sufficient enough to bring to his parched and searing wilderness the relief and release coming from those soothing words: "This day thou shalt be with me in Paradise." I choose to believe that the other thief, in spite of his to be understood befuddlement in wishing to be saved whether or no; an aggravated wish to be physically de-crossed whether by a miracle of his own descent, or otherwise, was also remembered. I, in my miscreant moments suggest that my Master saved him just for the "halibut." I believe that the twelve extra basketfuls of food collected at the multiplication lesson event involving a boy's lunch of loaves and fish, to be added fillip on his part to show that even his Father, through his Son's faith and the Father's innate abundance, his— both by definition and by the very nature of the phenomenon of divine opulence itself—wanted simply to "have some fun." The light touch is reminiscent of the time when the wine gave out at Cana, and turned the whole affair into a real party. Yea, even at the time of the great flood, a rainbow appeared at its subsidence. Why a useless rainbow? Oh, just to show that God loves us. Suffer him, please, the joy of throwing a kiss or two our way if he so chooses, After all, did not "God so love the world that he gave his only begotten Son"? And so we sing at our church:

> Lead me, guide me along the way,
> If you should leave me, I can but stray.
> Help me to walk each day with Thee;
> Lead me and guide me, lead me.

We need such a one to take out the interference as we carry the ball, as it were. He promises this assistance if we allow him to proffer it. The real miracle of the Red Sea happening is not its dramatic sensationalism but the simple fact that God is "Johnny on the spot" exactly when needed. So with the Christ of the Emmaeus road. Just when needed most, he appears to change shores of darkness into coasts of light. Not dramatically, but quietly, like the stars, really crashing worlds that, if out of orbit in contact with our world could smash it into a thousand pieces as if a sledgehammer were coming down upon a tinsel bulb. But the stars do not come that way, choosing rather to appear as twinkling lights to play with small boys who in familiar rhyme, inquire: "Twinkle, twinkle little star, how I wonder what you are?"

Granted that God helps those who help themselves, the empowerment that comes from knowing that one's help comes from him that made heaven and earth, simply has to put more "clobber" into one's "operation bootstrapping." The enabling power is generated through our own pure relationships with each other in concert with men's deepest needs lived out, and if need be died-out upon a demanding universal testing ground of a wrestling mat, where the endless contest is relieved, if not resolved, by the adversary's hip touch of our vulnerability—be it love of money, self, or pleasure —although the Achilles heel is bruised, the struggle goes on to find surcease only in the cemetery. And when the soul is free to act again in the next dimension, the real living experience is thus launched, unfolding into the eternality of his creation.

Jesus Christ as forerunner and precursor, thus, provides for me the rationale for sharing in the comforting hope found in John Greenleaf Whittier's wisdom as he writes:

> I know not what the future hath
>   Of marvel or surprise;
> Assured alone that life and death
>   God's mercy underlies.
>
> And if my heart and flesh are weak
>   To bear an untried pain;
> The bruised reed He will not break,
>   But strengthen and sustain.

> And so beside the silent sea
>   I wait the muffled oar;
> No harm from Him can come to me
>   On ocean or on shore.
>
> And Thou O Lord by whom are seen
>   Thy creatures as they be;
> Forgive me, if too close I lean
>   My human heart on Thee.
>
> I know not where His islands life
>   Their fronded palms in air;
> I only know I cannot drift
>   Beyond his love and care.

A thrilling account of the great pacemaker, at his reassuring best, is disclosed in that account in the book of 2 Samuel when David—the army's commander—was so ordered by God: "And let it be, when thou hearest the sound of a going in the tops of the mulberry trees, that then thou shalt bestir thyself: for then shall the Lord go out before thee, to smite the host of the Philistines." (2 Sam. 5:24). All that was left for God's army to do after that assurance was to move in and claim the territory.

So with me, as I trust in the Christ of God going out before me to blaze that kind of a trail to guarantee that kind of deliverance. Throughout this earthly journey, as he leads out from here, so will he lead out when my feet are about to "strike Zion."

"Then I won't be troubled any more. . . ."

Jesus Christ as Exemplar

At this point the Christ touch is most poignant for me. Ideally and idyllically, it is so expressed:

> There is a Green Hill far away,
> Without a city wall,
> Where the dear Lord was crucified,
> Who died to save us all.

> Oh dearly, dearly has He loved,
> And we must love Him too;
> And trust in His redeeming blood,
> And try His work to do.

The second epistle of John seems to be answering the inquiry, What is God like? with the reply, Look at Jesus Christ and see. The fourth chapter of the same letter tells us, scores of times, that God is love. This is the four letter word that holds together the whole human ball of wax. Its alienation, like the very air we breathe, we would all spontaneously resist. And although we are in an unlovely world, full of unlovely and unloving people, love is alone the only element available to preserve it. "Ah, Sweet Mystery of Life, at last I've found Thee!" Good, and faith, we'd better find it, and understand it, and know it for exactly what it is, and what miracles its application can accomplish.

An Irish policeman was approached by a lost Westerner who had drifted into Boston.

"Officer, please direct me to the Second Baptist Church," he implored.

"Faith and begorrah," came the reply, "I don't even know where the First Baptist Church is."

Love must be the fixed star toward which life's compass needle locating all the rest of our virtues must point. Nothing obstructs this northwest probe. "Here abideth faith, hope, and love; but the greatest of these is love." Thus wrote the apostle in that timeless essay on the subject, to the unlovely church at Corinth. We should thank God for the onery ways of that early membership. It provided the aetiology for the spawning of this masterpiece upon a subject which runs the gamut from petting in the back seat of a car all the way to Calvary.

The Lord Christ makes me know that we cannot be blessed with the authentic apprehension and understanding of this powerful dynamite without an exemplar who demonstrated what it was all

What Jesus Christ Means to Me

about, and how to apply it; for to him it was in very truth a weapon to conquer the forces of evil and might. He applied its touch in everything that he ever did, said, or thought. The forgiveness oozing through every pore of his physical and divine being was no accidental outpouring, but a contrived, structured, deliberately redemptive power play, designed to produce a gushing fountain for cleansing, which brought all of Christendom gapingly and gropingly trying to explain it, and leaving the believers singing:

> There is a Fountain filled with blood
> Drawn from Immanuel's veins;
> And sinners plunged beneath that flood,
> Lose all their guilty stains.

This is not slaughterhouse theology to me, but rather a song attempt to explain the elusive meaning of that great four letter word in all of its majestic, powerful, gloriously redemptive grandeur. The five-year-old boy could not even begin to understand it. If he for some reason were later to be compelled to try to fathom the depths of the miracle of the atonement and be required to tell of it, that would be easier for him to pick up mercury with a boxing glove. To this day the grandfather is unable to verbally cope with the full significance of the amazing paradox. Even so, it now is as clear as simplicity itself, when caught up into the swirl of the challenge to believe: God is love, Jesus Christ is totally filled with God. Jesus Christ is love. Yes, he is Lord, too; but Jesus Christ is love. There is no gnosticism here; rather, the discovery of an insight the acquisition of which so precious I would sooner die than surrender, of a loyalty the embracing of which so fervent I would sooner die than foreswear.

There is more. The demand, yea the absolute necessity to follow the example of Jesus Christ is now my burden whether I will it or no. The disdain shown by members of the cult of comfort which has by its very nature restrained the affluent from any attemp to change and seek to try to become sensitive to the hurts and cries of the less fortunate, now finds all of us on a collision course with doom; and our failure to disavow the impending peril which comes from a flabbiness which feeds upon the sloth which comes from the living of crossless lives, is demanding its pound of flesh. The tyranny of things has ordered our spiritual demise.

With our once rock-ribbed institutions crumbling into dust, and the wanton living (rather, dying) patterns making what happened in the decaying city-state of ancient Rome seem a Sunday School picnic by comparison; our "everything goes" culture is about to blow itself not only free from all restraint, but also completely apart upon the rocks of hedonistic, Epicurean license, with new and death-dealing experimental sexuality, with old bestial sensations searing the soul, and completely reducing to the viscosity of a dried up Post Toastie our moral, physical, spiritual vitality in one, all out, completely turned on blast of catastrophic finality. My, how we need the example of the Exemplar.

I do not believe this to be a post-Christian Era. I contend there is still enough true religion available; enough soul; enough charisma to bring about our salvation. If I thought the time was too far spent to reverse the traumatic trend, I should not have agreed to participate in the production of this book with so pious a title. How then are we to be equipped to get on with the urgent business of rescuing the perishing? By following his example, and by making use of an ever-present but finally appreciated device: salvation through the dynamics of the sparkling religious genius and ethos of the black church.

Now, before accusing me of hoisting myself up upon my own racial petard, I am immediately conscious of the need to at once turn to the example of the black preacher, ordained, educated, and renowned, who, like his Lord met crucifixion on April 4, 1968.

There is no doubt in my mind that Jesus Christ was his Exemplar throughout his controversial career, right up to the very earthly end of it. There is no doubt in my mind that similar sacrifice and offering up of life is the requirement that meets love's demand, if our relationships are, one, to be purified in a new experience of heretofore untried Christian adventure; two, to be restored to a level of high dedication by a fresh memory of the preciousness of the worth of the old personal associations we once held, as the challenges from the satanic Predator are courageously and successfully parried; and, three, to find maturity in a saving recognition of the "high cost of loving" as seen in our responses to the broken fellowship between ourselves and ourselves, ourselves and our brothers, ourselves and our beloved Lord.

No martyr attempting by his death to bind up broken relationships has ever gone to the gibbet, pyre, or the cross unexpectedly. The Master realized in Gethsemane that his time had finally come. Dr. Martin Luther King expressed the conviction in the last speech before Memphis that in all likelihood his trek to that city would prove to be a "via dolorosa." I talked to Malcolm X on the Wednesday before the Sunday he was slain; and the conversation was full of portents of his soon to be assassination. Abraham Lincoln on April 12 saw his image in a coffin in the White House; on April 14 the vision became a fact. In truth, Jesus Christ himself is not so much a part of history as ploughed into history, with the cross as ploughshare.

What can all of this mean, save the hard realization that there is no redemption without creative pain, when one sets out to restore broken relationships among the brethren; that whenever one moves radically to serve the ends of the poor and down-trodden, the establishment will hurt, if not actually eliminate him.

Such an insight frightens me, and naturally so, since there is not a martyr bone in my "Boddie," but Bob Wallace and the Hopevale martyrs will probably tell us, should the opportunity be theirs to do so, "there is no other way, but to trust and obey." I am ever haunted by the fact that

> "There is only one door
>   For Thomas More."

Whatever influenced the martyrs to become such was surely something akin to the behavior pattern set by the great Exemplar. The Christ present in the midst is doubtless what explains the holy outpouring from those whose immortal names are etched upon the sacred list relating to sacrifices from the time of the incidents which gave peculiar meaning to the Catacombs and the Lorraine Hotel.

To sing, "Lord I Want to Be A Christian" is to cause pause if one hearkens to the words of Dietrich Bonhoefer, who was put to death in a Nazi prison: The call to Christian discipleship is a call to die.

To out love your adversary means to out die him also. T. R. Glover's famous statement truthfully reminds us that the early Christians survived as a strong movement because the capacity of the devotees "to out live, out think, and out die" their pagan contemporaries. I hasten to add and out love them too. This smacks of the way of life as followed by that of my Exemplar, the capstone of my striving, as I seek to discover how, in his Holy Name, I can ever be like him.

Thomas a'Kempis finds his spiritual catharsis writing about imitation of Christ. But Liza Doolittle more importantly shakes our complacency with "Don't talk of love; Show me!" She comes too close to what I hear my Exemplar saying for my full enjoyment and appreciation of "My Fair Lady."

Worship to many is the scapegoat upon which they saddle the burden on their moral inertia. This is perhaps the reason behind his insistent and persistent "follow me" instead of worship me. He still presses: "Follow me and I will make you." But if following means all the way to Calvary for us, most of us will forsake him, for we simply lack the will to commit and submit to that demanding kind of obedience. My haunting fear is that I am among them. I feel the lack of sufficient, soul stamina, character, and integrity to join him in such holy state of martyrdom, as it were.

As long as this condition prevails, and it must be resolved soon, as the time is short and the choice to die with him may yet and soon come to me, I shall be confounded by the Babelian ways that characterize the conduct of our smitten race of hitherworldly humans, caught up in our awful humanity, as, although speaking the same language cannot understand each other. Is there any percentage in praying for another Pentecost, where, although speaking in different tongues people understood each other? Is such divine communication possible for us save as the Holy Spirit dwells among us? Christ in the form of the Holy Spirit, as Our Exemplar, moving into the core of our being may yet forestall Armageddon.

Life's Greatest Astonishment

I cannot fully grasp the ultimately true meaning of his love for me, this One whose coming split time in two: but I shall never stop seeking to know more, and more, and more about him. And as my knowledge increases, I shall pray that my will to obey him shall take hold, and become strong; and that by my example someone else will come to know him as life's greatest astonishment.

When in the face of my shortcomings, in the light of his perfection I am prone to torture myself with feelings of guilt, I set out to try to do some decent thing to, for, or with somebody. I feel better at once.

If there is a strange inefficiency about working in the kingdom's vineyard where everyone regardless of the number of hours logged receives one farthing for his labor, such inequity is compensated for when I contemplate upon the one who paid it all for me; and into whose loving and judicious care my life has been placed. This sort of conduct is all that kept my ancestors from extinction. If it was effective for them, then, I have got to believe in its efficacy for my condition now and commend to members of the now generation a faith formula which not only expects, but remembers. To accept it may yet be a way to at least tip our worlds a hair's breadth closer to a common dawn as we seek together to bridge the infernal gap. Should memory be eschewed then I can only turn it over to Jesus Christ, Superstar, who really is what they (including me) say he is: Redemptor, Preemptor, Precursor, Exemplar.

If this is telling it like it was rather than like it is, please forgive; and may we at least let him who is our dwelling place throughout all generations, move in to possess us, wherever, however, and whenever he is able. Are we willing?

6 WHAT CHRIST MEANS TO ME
Edward V. Hill

(AS TOLD TO LINDA ELIZABETH RANEY)

HALLELUJAH JESUS! Discovery! Understanding! Purpose! Power! Productivity! Calling! Family! Resource! Fantastic! *This* and *much more* is what Christ means to me!!

I can only thank him and praise him for the tremendous nouns and thrilling adjectives he has filled my life with.

A Pot of Heavenly Gold

First on the list and foremost in my thoughts is the word "discovery." It was at an early age that I discovered Christ as my Savior. The fact that he loved me enough to die for me personally motivated me to accept his free gift of living forever. This was a great discovery! Then there followed big discoveries and little discoveries, simple discoveries and complex discoveries. But for me as a Negro, a certain trip across the South in the early fifties was perhaps one of the greatest discoveries of all.

As a freshman at Prairie View, a part of the Texas A. and M. system, I was actively involved in the Baptist Student Union. The National BSU Convention for Negroes, held in Nashville, Tennessee, was a highlight of the year. Much to my pleasure, I was one of two students selected to go. White students had raised the money. That was okay with me, as I viewed it as an act of pity on their part to a lesser human being; or at best a chance to ease their guilty conscience. But then real trouble began!

The trip through the South was by car—three whites and two Negroes traveling together. I had no idea how we'd eat or how we'd sleep. So great was my anxiety and hatred over how the trip might turn out that I almost backed out entirely.

The whites didn't care—the white Christian didn't care. In all my experience I had never seen a white man stand up for a black man and never felt I would.

"We'll be traveling together," Dr. Howard, the director of our trip spoke up. "If there isn't a place where all of us can eat—none of us will eat. If there's not a place all of us can sleep—none of us will sleep."

That was all he said—but it was enough! For the first time in my life I had met a white man who was Christian enough to take a stand with a Christian black man.

The trip across country was a tense one for me. The white people had the right attitude. But in the midst of their love and concern, their impartiality and total acceptance, my hate and "I'll show you" attitude stuck out like a sore thumb.

I had thought it was *only* the white folks that needed a change of heart. But now I saw myself in the same condition in which I had seen the white community—active in church, speaking of God; but justifying my own un-Christlike attitudes. The error was tilted in my favor. The finger was pointing straight at me!

I was about to discover the third world.

So on the trip and at the meetings I discovered there was another world. There was the Negro world. There was the white world. Now there was a third world—the Christian World.

What is it?

The third world is a place where men of every color, every race, and every language love one another, stand by one another, and sacrifice for one another whatever the cost!

It is a by-product.

It is a symptom.

It is an experience.

It is the love of God produced in a man to the extent that the color of a man's skin makes no difference.

It is the *result* of allowing Jesus Christ to be "top priority" in a man's life!

And at this point of discovery, I committed my entire life to Christ. I invited Him to take control, to take the reigns of my life. I would no longer fight for just my own cause. I would fight for *His* cause, along with my white brothers and sisters. And with His strength, His wisdom, His power, His guidance—we *were* going to win!

A Great Discovery!

To Understand

Christ means to me "understanding."

There was a time when I hated the white man! Among the generalities there were some specifics for my rage. First of all the white man was a hypocrite. He talked equality in the Declaration of Independence, and piously in the churches across the land, but lived with partialities in his daily life.

Secondly he was selfish and egotistical. He had designed and perpetuated a system that favored his own skin color and short-circuited mine. And I resented the white people's belief that the Negro was just trying to become white. Such self-centeredness on the part of the white man was detestable to me.

Third and most important, I hated the white man because he gave me a position beneath my capabilities. The frustrating roadblocks—"You can't eat in my kitchen"; "You can't drink from my fountain"; "You can't go to my school"; "You can't handle my job"; "You can't even urinate in my pot"; were constantly there to remind me of my "white-people imposed" position. A position they would not let me bypass. I could not bypass!

But God gave me understanding!

He opened my eyes.

He showed me that segregation is not from God. It is from the devil. Therefore any man participating in it is doing the devil's job.

Furthermore, since the problem originated in a spiritual sphere, it couldn't be settled by just earthly means. Legislature, decrees, marches and riots—these can't change the heart of man. Only God can conquer a segregated heart: first through conversion (a turnabout to Christ): secondly through the "understanding" God gives to men who seek the truth.

Segregation in Africa, in China, in Vietnam, in India, in Russia, in America—all the devil's work pitting man against man—can be resolved only at the cross!

This is the "understanding" Christ gives to me.

Purpose Anyone?

But Jesus Christ, besides revealing new discoveries and giving understanding, offers me purpose. I'll never forget my purpose as a youth—to win Grand Champion of the Hog Division at the County Fair!

My first hog was a "Sears and Roebuck hog." Now a "Sears and Roebuck hog" is one where the boy is given a pig with the understanding that the boy will raise the pig, breed it, then give someone else the pick of the litter. This was a choice opportunity as the pig was the finest around. To be considered, a boy had to write a paper explaining what he would do with the pig if he had the opportunity. I spent a month on the paper.

I'll never forget the morning I was awarded the pig. I had less than a week to prepare for it. But it was worth all the effort! When the State Fair opened I won the Grand Champion! The only trouble was that when paying time came around the white boy's hog paid $3.00 a pound; mine paid $.50 a pound.

My purpose began to change.

It doesn't take a man long—white or black—knocking his head against those kinds of odds to figure out that something somewhere is wrong. It seemed I was faced with two choices. Either I would accept the status quo, passively fitting into the mold someone else made for me, or I would resist it. I chose the latter!

My new purpose was to fight for the dignity of the Negro. There was no bitterness at first. But slowly there began to build within me a hatred—an earnest hatred that remained and increased to an unbearable point because there was little or nothing I could do about the situation.

This purpose "to bring dignity to the Negro" continued with me when I entered the "third world." But it was soon brought into the proper perspective. Now, my main purpose would be to bring others into the third world. For the emphasis in life is neither the black world or the white world—but the kingdom of God! This is something all races must work together for.

Since that experience, this purpose of bringing men to Jesus Christ has been the consuming desire in my heart. It is not a partial answer such as integration, or a temporary solution such as legislation. Neither is it a work that deals with the surface changes in man only: more important than a man's circumstances is the attitude of his heart!

My purpose now is greater than any environmental change I may bring about. My purpose now is hitting at the root problem, not merely the surface symptoms. My purpose now is introducing men to Jesus Christ! Because a proper relationship with Jesus Christ is the key to the total and perfect answer to every one of life's dilemmas—great or small! And it is something you won't understand until you've experienced it.

But Christ did more for me than to leave me with a purpose. He provided the energy and the resources to carry it out. And this is why Jesus Christ means to me "Power."

Jesus Power

It was a dark day in the summer of '65. The Watts area of Los Angeles was being rioted by thousands of earnest young blacks. Instantly the news media was on the scene painting an even darker picture of the week's events. It left parts of the city in shambles. It left many frightened and disillusioned. It left the Christians of Watts on their knees!

"Lord, this isn't helping your cause. This isn't helping our people. We're waiting on you now, Lord. Show us what to do."

If you have the faith—God has the power!

As one minister put it, "Let's make Watts burn again! This time . . . for God!

By June of 1966 amazing things had happened in response to prayers and the power of God. The first summer after the riot we enrolled 902 in Bible School with more than 200 professed decisions for Christ. The second summer after the riot we enrolled 4,928 in Bible School with more than 500 "new faiths" reported. Twenty-eight local churches and twenty-two mission stations were left glowing with the thrill of the presence and power of God.

And God is still at work in tremendous ways.

If you have the faith—God has the Power!

A Life That Counts!

Productivity follows. Christ means to me—productivity. Because of Christ my life is accomplishing something! Because of Christ my life is counting for something! Now!

Let me describe to you what I call productive. Get someone into my church. Well, that may be a start, but I don't term it production. Get someone to walk the aisle. Well, that too may be a start, but not necessarily real production.

Find a life—see it changed by forgiveness and commitment to Christ, trained in the Scriptures, sharing good news with others, being a stable person in the community. That's real production!

Take Arthur Thomas for instance. At age 45 Arthur, a Negro, was a discouraged man. He had quit his job. Finding himself at home one morning he tuned to a Los Angeles radio station. I was speaking that morning of the change Christ can make in a man's life. "It was your enthusiasm," Arthur commented later, "and your final statement 'Man's *only* hope is in Christ' that really started me thinking."

Two weeks later, Arthur joined with us at the church—a changed man. He had given his life to Christ.

A new job opened to Arthur as superintendent of the clothing department at Tehachapi Prison. The "new" Arthur was anxious to impart his "faith in Christ" to the men at Tehachapi. His love and concern caught on quickly with the men. The inmates soon sought him out for advice and direction. On a number of occasions he was able to quell prison riots and encourage needed reform. But always he was a testimony of the changing power of Jesus Christ. Two years later, in light of his outstanding work, he was offered the position of warden.

What's he doing today? At age 49, Arthur D. Thomas has just enrolled at seminary!

Brother Carter is another, Sister Jones is another . . . and I could go on and on! And I have only Christ to praise for it. Jesus Christ has made my life productive!

Unlimited

Jesus Christ means to me "Calling."

In the Negro world there are limits. In the white world there are limits. To the man called of God there are no limits!

During high school graduation exercises, Negro students were admonished to continue their education. Someday they'd return and be the school principal, the pastor of a church, or a county agent. As for me, my "big dream" was to succeed the local agriculture teacher. We were also admonished to get ourselves clean, rid ourselves of disease, establish our culture, rise socially, get rich, and . . . yet after all this, the white man couldn't fully accept us. We were limited by what we were.

Naturally, our community never allowed this self-improvement idea to die. It was the carrot constantly kept before the mule. Work on. Improve yourself.

Exit ivory tower!

However, at about age twelve, when the boys returned from World War II, I learned, as did many Negroes, the hypocrisy of the "self-improvement gospel" passed our way. There's another world out there, they told us. A world where Negro people, though imperfect, are accepted. We also learned from them that in other parts of the world all whites were not perfect. Some were not clean. Some were not educated. Some were filled with disease. In fact that was happening in some parts of our own country.

Then we heard rumors from all over the country that Negroes who had prepared themselves—cleaned and educated themselves—were being turned away from jobs and opportunities in favor of a white man of equal, sometimes inferior, preparation.

The picture was becoming all too clear.

Aspirations and possibilities available to whites were limited to whites. Limited to whites! But what if *I* wanted to be the President of the United States? What if *I* wanted to be the richest businessman around? It seemed that, in the white world and in the Negro world systems, color was one huge hurdle that stood in my way.

A man "called of God."

But somehow—a man "called of God" is able to jump the hurdles that make other men quit—even the hurdle of color and race. Such has been my testimony year after year. In spite of all the difficulties and impossibile situations God has always seen me through.

When God tells a man to "step outside," he always opens the door.

One sure thing to help you keep going when things get rough is to make sure you've started right. My "calling from God"—a solid beginning—has sustained me in times of pressure, and been my cause for much joy all through my life.

Keep the Home Fires Burning

In a day when most families are falling a part, it is interesting to see—in fact, it is a wonder to behold—the way Christ can "cement" a family together. This is why Christ means to me "family."

God—the author of marriage and family—first brought into my life a beautiful little thing called "Jane." She was only seventeen at the time. I'm so glad I let Jesus Christ order the events as far as my marriage is concerned. By no stretch of the imagination could I have made a better choice. We were married five years later.

My wife is my baby and my queen. Actually, she is a dual personality. On the one hand, she is a very intelligent woman. She has a master's degree in health education and a bachelor's in the science of nursing. But on the other hand, she is a little dumb country girl. And this is the thing I like most about her. She's intelligent where she needs to be intelligent, but 90% of the time she's just this little helpless individual lamb that needs somebody to rescue her.

There's a lot of "soul" in our marriage!

Then God brought along Norva, age 15 now. And Edward, age four. Both have brought much joy and satisfaction into our home.

But God gives us another Family, too. This is the family of Christians all over the world. Every country has some of my family. Some from every language speak of belonging to my family; God's special family—made up of those who love him and know his forgiveness through Christ.

Knowing I'm part of this family is a great joy and a great responsibility. It's one of the many things that come to mind when I recall "What Christ Means to Me."

Need a Supply?

Jesus Christ means "Resource."

Prior to my college days I entertained the most interesting education. My twelve school years employed only four teachers—my agriculture teacher.* By present-day standards the school that gave me my basic training had "no right to exist!"

In light of this meager background and in spite of it I have been called on to advise governors and statesmen, senators, Presidents, and foreign ambassadors. I have headed many boards including the Housing Commission, the Los Angeles Fire Commission, Urban League, the Mayor's Committee on Economic Opportunities; organized the Opportunities Industrialization, been a board member with NAACP, Governor's Advisory Committee, Western Baptist Convention, Foreign Mission Board, National Sunday School Association, Baptist World Youth Conference. In addition I have been the guest speaker for many colleges and Christian organizations including the University of California at Berkeley, the University of Southern California, Campus Crusade for Christ, the Billy Graham Association, and many others.

How?

The question is—how?

The answer is Jesus Christ!!

Amidst challenges and difficulties when my advice and instruction have been crucial to the community I have—through and by means of Jesus Christ—been *made* "able."

He gives wisdom.

He gives strength.

He gives knowledge.

He gives guidance.

He gives encouragement.

He gives even His angels to be at my disposal.

It's Fantastic!

Finally the word that sums it all up. What does Christ mean to

---

*We had no counsellors, no experts, little or no teaching equipment, secondhand books, no science labs, no typewriters, a wood stove which I tended—a combination of few essentials and no extras.

me? He means *fantastic!* Fantastic living! Fantastic opportunities! Fantastic hopes! Fantastic everything!

"Eye hasn't seen
"Ear hasn't heard
"Neither has man begun to understand
"The fantastic things God has prepared for those who love Him."
—1 Corinthians 2:9 (Paraphrased)

It's Fantastic!!!
And that is what Jesus Christ means to me.

7 WHAT JESUS MEANS TO ME
Manuel L. Scott

With massive earnestness I intend to make crystal clear "What Jesus means to me." When this endeavor is ended, it will be proper to remark as did the Queen of Sheba concerning the wisdom of Solomon—"The half has not been told." Jesus Christ, whether viewed in the perspective of personal encounters or the process of history is, in Pauline language, "God's unspeakable gift." No skill of tongue or pen, no inner sensibilities, no sharpness of intellect, nor keenness of imagination is sufficient to fully reveal the riches of Jesus Christ. It is not surprising that the Evangelist who penned the Gospel of John all but exaggerated his conclusion by saying, "And there are also many other things which Jesus did, the which, if they should be written every one, I suppose that even the world itself could not contain the books that should be written" (John 21:25).

This testimony is just beginning and already I am in a mood somewhat like the lad who with much effort and determination attempted to draw a picture of Jesus Christ, but finally gave up. On being asked by his teacher why he didn't complete the venture he replied, "He is too beautiful to paint." Nevertheless, in response to a request and in obedience to our Lord's mandate to witness, I proceed to set down in reasonable order my personal Jesusology.

The reader should keep two things, among many, in mind while reflecting on my journey with Jesus. First of all, being a Christian pulpiteer I am assailed by the powerful temptation to preach, that is to tell what Jesus ought to mean to me and to others. I have put forth a rugged and vigorous effort to resist this enticement. It should also be kept in mind that because such a statement is intrinsically autobiographical some of it may sound like self-praise or strutting pride if casually considered. The matter of my self-estimate is worded with competence and conclusiveness in those familiar lines of the apostle Paul, "I count not myself to have apprehended: but this one thing I do, forgetting those things which are behind, and reaching forth unto those things which are before, I press toward the mark for the prize of the high calling of God in Christ Jesus."

Rugged honesty and responsible objectivity compels me to observe that this matter of "What Jesus means to me," has a gloomy side as well as a glory side. This walk through life with Jesus as registered in my experiences is paradoxical and ambivalent. There are gains, but there are also losses. There is healing, but there is also hurt. There is succor, but there is also demand. There is compensation, but there is also cost. There is peace, but there is also warfare. There is joy, but there are also tears. There is freedom, but there is also bondage. There are triumphs, but there is also tragedy.

Dietrich Bonhoeffer's much talked about work, *The Cost of Discipleship,* calls attention to this stretch of desert and barren land in our pilgrimage with Jesus. Another has aptly accentuated the obstacle courses confronting adherents of the Christian religion in saying, "Jesus promised his followers two things; he would be with them and they would get in trouble." We seers and sayers never tire of saying, "The blood of the martyrs is the seed of the church." I have washed my robe in the blood of the Lamb, but I have also borne my "burdens in the heat of the day." I did come to "Jesus as I was, weary, worn, and sad," and I did find "in him a resting place and he has made me glad." I have also come through trials and tribulation. I have often prayed with the poet:

> Just as I am, though tossed about,
> With many a conflict, many a doubt;
> Fightings within and fears without,
> O Lamb of God, I come.

I am not just a beneficiary of his blood. I am a bearer of his cross. No wonder the New Testament speaks of the Christian life in terms of "taking up a cross," "taking a yoke upon you," "suffering with him," "light afflictions," and "dying daily." Whenever I take my hat off to a card-carrying Christian, I know I make a "salute to a sufferer."

Now I move to the glory side of this walk with Jesus. To begin with Jesus Christ is a personal and intimate friend of mine. This relationship with Christ is an interpersonal one. To be a Christian as reflected in my experience is to know not merely in what one believes, but in whom one believes. It was someone, not something, who confronted me when just a boy on the streets of Waco, Texas, saved me from sin, spoke to me gently, and "with compassion folded me close to his bosom." It is a dynamic person, not some vague principle and impersonal philosophy which claims my supreme allegiance, on whom I cast my main dependence, and from whom I get my deepest joy. It is a character [Jesus] not a concept who is the crux of my Christian journey. Christmas and Easter are highly significant days for me. The former commemorates the personal arrival of Jesus. The latter celebrates his personal survival which renders him available to all and inaccessible to none.

In the fifteenth chapter of the Gospel of John Jesus addressed to those first disciples some words of warm comfort and counsel. "Henceforth I call you not servants; for the servant knoweth not what his lord doeth: but I have called you friends; for all things that I have heard of my Father I have made known unto you." These words belong to every believer. Implied in them is appealing news that the believer's union with Christ is one in which the essential ingredients of responsible friendship are embraced. He shares with us his secrets and his strength. He is always for us and never against us. He is persistent in providing us with survival benefits. He keeps open the lines of communication and the lanes of progress. He solicits unbroken comradeship. He charges us to keep his commandments and commission. He cherishes supping with us as we sup with him.

I am writing these lines while having a general checkup at Mayo Clinic in Rochester. Invariably, all the waitresses in the coffee shop place on the back of my food check these words, "Thank you and have a good day, Mary Jane." In this way these public servants add to the eating transaction a touch of the personal and a gesture of friendship. All of Christ's disciples are endowed by him with this dimension of the personal and friendly.

Moreover, Jesus is to me a "meeter of needs and a solver of problems," as well as the supplier of many of my wants. I am very much aware that many claimants of the Christian faith would consider this religious utilitarianism. They would accuse me of reducing Christianity to a mere "opiate for the masses"; "a chloroform mask in which the weak and ignorant take refuge"; "a bread and butter faith"; and a "foxhole religion." Nevertheless, length of time and frequency of experience have not dimmed or diminished my conviction that Christ is all that I stated above. It fortifies me as I reflect on Jesus' memorable words in regard to neediness. "Therefore, take no thought, saying, What shall we eat? or, What shall we drink? or, Wherewithal shall we be clothed? (For after all these things do the Gentiles seek) for your heavenly Father knoweth that ye have need of all these things. But seek ye first the kingdom of God, and his righteousness; and all these things shall be added unto you." I am made all the stronger when I ponder Paul's saying; "But my God shall supply all your need according to his riches in glory by Christ Jesus." These two Scripture passages are literally "lights unto my pathway and lamps unto my feet." Incessantly incidents and events are vivid on my voyage which illustrate and illuminate these Bible intonations. In all of those realms where life is most real he provides all that is necessary and much that is desired: in the physical, economic, social, intellectual, moral, and spiritual departments.

I never cease to marvel at the abundant and ample way Christ has met my material need and that of my wife and six children. The New Testament asserts that "they which preach the gospel should live of the gospel." This is signally true in my case without the slightest variation of derivation. No other vocation or avocation has been a consumer of my energies and efforts or a monetary compensator. Mrs. Thelma Scott has been free to fully assume her role as mother, wife, and homemaker without interference from work on the outside. This freedom and efficiency in my wife explains to a large degree the desirable traits of discipline, decency, and dignity which I, thankfully and humbly, see manifested in my children. At our house we've always had bread and to spare. We are far from being rich, but we've never been in rags. I don't mean to imply that I have been without bills or economic battles. I've even gotten behind and been compelled to borrow; though never to beg. However, in every difficult eventuality Christ has set before me an "open door."

I rejoice when I reflect on the many-splendored manner in which Jesus provides for my intellectual needs. My achievements in formal education are painfully below my aspiration. I believe that "they who preach" in an age of science and rationality should attain the highest in organized and systematized academics, (a PhD, if possible.) The discipline and development which are compulsive and obligatory in school are seldom elected by those outside the academic community. In spite of limitations in formal education I am an aggressive and relentless adventurer in the kingdom of thought. I find it difficult to warm my heart without commanding my head. I have an unappeasable impatience with intellectual mediocrity when something better is possible. I am dedicated to the proposition that in the long run that cause will triumph which has the collaboration and consuming concern of the ablest intellectuals providing these giant minds are spiritualistic and appreciate authentic ethical values. I think H. G. Wells is far within the mark when he says, "History is a race between education and catastrophe." Samuel Du Bois Cook, in his introduction to Benjamin A. Mays' book, *Born to Rebel,* has succinctly and summarily expressed my sentiment respecting the role of reason and the mission of mind. "The old ship of reason," he writes, "while not without handicaps in negotiating the turbulent waters of the contemporary world, is not completely disabled. It is a good and secure ship—built especially for the troubled water of the human journey. It is the most reliable ship in the whole harbor of civilization. It is old but even young." There is no substitute for rational and experimental exploration and evaluation of alternative conditions, possibilities, and consequences, the cool calculation of the probable consequences of each option, the counting of the cost, and the bringing of what is out of sight into view.

In ways too numerous to tell, the Master has accommodated my mind and make. Repeatedly Jesus has confronted me with those challenges, characters, and situations which gave cultivation and sophistication to my intellect. In high school I was privileged to participate in the debating club and declamatory contests as well as preside over the student body. The church of my childhood, the Toliver Chapel Baptist Church in Waco, Texas, assigned to me responsibilities which under ordinary circumstances would have been reposed in the hands of the more mature. Throughout my college days at Bishop, now in Dallas, Texas, I was able to remain on the honor roll, encouraged by the faculty and inspired by students of like dispositions. The congregation of the Calvary Baptist Church at Los Angeles, which has honored me to be its pastor for twenty-two years, has had among its membership those persons in whom the love of learning was vibrant and vigorous and who stimulated the leadership to be both a scholar and a saint. Members of this make bought me books by brilliant authors from various disciplines, mouthed thanks for a message which had caused me to "toil like a miner under a landslide," responded to my preaching with something other than emotions, and encouraged me to do as our Lord commanded John on Patmos, "What thou seest, write in a book."

Most recently the Master has continued and expanded my intellectual venture by the many invitations to speak coming from the Southern Baptist Convention. This society of many saints, numbering more than eleven million, sponsoring and nurturing colleges, seminaries, and universities, and peppered with first-class preachers and fraternal prophets, has come to my kingdom "for such a time as this." I might have been lost in the local, littered with a theology all too liberal, laden with lethargy, buried beneath the rubbish of the routine, enslaved by the ethnic, and frustrated by a feeling of futility, had not it been for the creative encounter with this Southern Baptist community. Southern Baptist handed me a "new situation" and a "new affection" from which I received the stimulus to read, write, and reach for an unprecedented range of relevance and relationships. More than once I have left Los Angeles all but convinced that I had neither the courage nor the competence to continue my favorite and fundamental pursuits. After meeting, however, with this Southern Baptist brotherhood my strength was renewed and my departed confidence restored. I have little noted nor will I long remember what I have done for them, but I can never forget what they have done for me.

Such helps for my mind would be explained by many people as the fruits of fate, the benevolence of blind chance, or just amiable accidents or incidents in the evolutionary process. Not so; as for me I have been aided by the ceaseless energy and matchless genius of Jesus Christ.

With equal jubilation I submit that Christ is a meeter of my moral and social needs. Among my deepest persuasions (major ingredients in my anthropology) is the idea that man is a moral as well as an intellectual being whose destiny is determined to a large degree by the rightness or wrongness of his actions and attitudes. I am equally convinced that man is a gregarious character, a social being as well as an individual whose fortunes and future are inter-connected with his inter-human relations; his being fit to live with. Jesus Christ is my chief resource person, main mentor and model in my struggle for moral fitness and social competence. Christ is by constitution fitted for those fine lines in Micah. "He hath shewed thee, O man, what is good; and what doth the Lord require of thee, but to do justly, and to love mercy, and to walk humbly with thy God?"

As I reflect on Jesus' socio-moral significance it rushes to mind that he has enabled me to live respectably in spite of poverty and without rancor or revenge in the midst of racial antipathy and inequality. I was born and bred in a poverty pocket. I discovered America in the South where the pressure of poverty and iniquity pressed against a black man's neck. I know the giant agonies of the ghetto and the dangers of dark streets. I comprehend easily what it means to be "culturally deprived and economically underprivileged." I can do a thesis on the hardship of the hard-core poor. I have first hand experience with police brutality and political injustice. I know what it means to be under paid and never praised. I sold apples as a boy for a penny on the bucket; worked all day and made a dime. I delivered mail for a white postman, over a half day's work, and was given a nickel for the daily run. I bear in my being the marks of a people who lived as slaves for almost 250 years and as second class citizens for a century. I was separated by the system and structures of segregation from those institutions which could have tutored and tailored me best. Nevertheless, I have been able to live by dent of Christian discipleship in what another has called, "respectable poverty." In respectable poverty there is a willingness to work, an impatience with indolence and a dislike for laziness. In respectable poverty there is a penchant and proclivity for earning an honest dollar, a stubborn refusal to steal or rob, or be parasitically supported by the sweat of another's face. In respectable poverty there is the disposition to share, to "cast one's bread upon the water," and to engage in costly and dangerous altruism. In respectable poverty there is the wisdom that works and waits for the rising of a new day, a freedom from satisfaction with wants that needle and needs which are a nuisance.

In like manner Jesus is to me a deterrent against my becoming a victim of those vicious "V's"—vengeance, vandalism, and violence—which apparently track the misused minorities and socially mained. In sitting at his feet I have learned that thee is no vitality in vengeance, no help in hate, no profit in pillaging and plundering the properties of another and no abiding victory in violence. In feeding on his teachings I have waxed strong in the conviction that the love-ethics "exalts a nation" and its counterpart "is a reproach to any people."

A short while before the current "Black Revolt" in America I read Howard Thurman's *Jesus and the Disinherited*. With rare vividness and charisma this book riveted attention on the fact that Jesus while in flesh was a member of the downtrodden and deprived of the population. The immediate "blood of his blood and bone of his bone" bore their "burdens in the heat of the day." Nevertheless, Jesus was not bitten by the bug of bitterness. He did not revel in the rhetoric of revenge. He did not belong so fully to the Jewish race that he bowed out of membership in the human race. He did not take lightly and indiscretely the fruits of forgiveness. He did not mobilize militarily as a means of securing rights and freedom. Mark you well, he was no preserver of the useless and evil past. He was not neutralized by the giant magnitude of the social crisis. He was no "Uncle Tom" or "yes-man" cringing and crawling before the power structure. He was no opportunist, exploiting every moment, movement, and matter for personal gains. He was no surviver of the status quo, lacking in creativity and dynamics for change. He was a radical, a rebel, and a revolutionist, initiating and activating moral and spiritual forces to wreck evil systems and structure and reconstruct a world of humans who live in harmony and mutual helpfulness and trust. I hazard the assertion and prophesy that apart from Christ and his way, mankind shall have no more success with its plan for peace than those who attempted in the long ago to build a stairway to the stars.

Finally, and this is far from being least, Christ is the meeter of my spiritual needs. That we are all citizens of two worlds is an incontestable fact. Our days are spelled out and our destiny is designed by dualistic factors and forces. The visible and the invisible, the passing and the permanent, the mundane and the metaphysical, the actual and the possible, the known and the unknown, the immanent and the transcendent, give character and content to the "life we prize." It is to this world of the spiritual that Jesus' mission, message, and make speak with unique and unparalleled potency and pentinence.

The spiritual concerns of man have since time began centered in three questions: Is there a God? What is he like? and What does he will for my life that will insure a satisfying relation with him? Jesus is for me the clear, correct,and continuing answer to these questions.

I am tremendously impressed by the fact that he never argued the existence of God. He merely earthed and fleshed out his certainty that there was another being beside human being. He even went far enough to declare that he was, not like other men merely identified with the supreme and supernatural one, but identical with him. "I and my Father are one" is his mystical and bold affirmation. Whenever God-talk is done or God-questions are raised, I think immediately of Jesus Christ. Whenever I am confronted with atheistic temptations that would have me "play the fool (say in my heart, "there is no God,"), my theistic faith is tempered and sustained by the glory and goodness that flashes in the face of Jesus.

Likewise, Jesus has addressed himself to my spiritual needs by revealing God's essential nature and fundamental disposition. John 1:18 sums up my sentiment. "No man hath seen God at any time: the only begotten Son, which is in the bosom of the Father, he hath

What Jesus Means to Me

declared him." For those who, like Philip, implored me to show them God, I respond in the words of Jesus, "Believest thou not that I am in the Father, and the Father in me? the words that I speak unto you I speak not of myself: but the Father that dwelleth in me, he doeth the works." "He that hath seen me hath seen the Father." Because I know Jesus my theology includes the idea that God is good. On one occasion Christ exclaimed, "There is none good but God." I confess that at times in an effort to reconcile the fact of God's goodness and his all-powerfulness, I am bewildered. The presence of so many brutal facts and bad realities leave me with answers which fall short. Nevertheless, I am contented in the realization that God is not omni-casual. There are other actors whose derelictions and devious ways enter into the drama of life. Because of my encounter with Jesus one of my deepest persuasions is that God loves me. John 3:16, which mirrors the gospel in miniature, begins with "God so loved the world." I am consoled in the assurance that God wills to benefit me and possess me. God cares for me and is careful with me. God calculates his moves so as to realize my noblest possibilities.

Moreover, my fellowship with Christ bestows on me the blessed confidence that God answers prayer. As for me, the worthwhile is accomplished in this world by three exercises, namely, thinking, working, and praying. The prayer acts of Jesus provides ample evidence that prayer is not monologue, but dialogue—a conversation between God and me. Jesus also illustrated for me that I can pray with definiteness and as a petitioner. I can ask God for specific needs and wants. Jesus has tutored me in the awareness that the answer from God is sometimes "no." He has enriched my prayer philosophy with the consciousness that I should always pray with importunity and undiscouragable expectancy. Jesus confronts me with the painful challenge to pray for those who despitefully use me.

The last question in this trio of spiritual concerns is one of magnificent urgency and monumental decisiveness. The highest good in life and the chief goal of history is to know and do the will of God. It is not strange that Jesus taught us to pray, "Thy will be done." It is not surprising that he said to the woman from Samaria, "My meat is to do the will of him that sent me." It is understandable why he prayed earnestly and in agony, "Father, all things are possible unto thee; take away this cup from me: nevertheless not what I will, but what thou wilt." It is rewarding to reflect that among the wonders of creation only man is endowed with the awful and dangerous freedom to defy the will of our Maker. This inability to discern and penchant for disobeying the will of God explains at least in part the chaotic and calamitous condition of the human family.

I have learned from Jesus that God's will involves allocating priority to his will, putting his purposes and program above self and society. Jesus has also led me to believe that God's will includes following Jesus, reproducing his mind and morals in our everyday living. "If any man would come after me," so Christ enjoins us, "let him deny himself, take up his cross and follow me." Many who have no stock in the Christian corporation are quick to admit that we are all better persons when we succeed in placing our footprints "in his steps." The goodness and glad tiding are also broken to me through Jesus that the will of God consists in believing in Jesus, the saving efficacy of his shed blood, the power of his resurrection, the endowments of his intercession, the inescapability of his final judgment and the glory of his return.

> Blessed assurance, Jesus is mine!
> Oh, what a foretaste of glory divine!
> Heir of salvation, purchase of God,
> Born of His Spirit, washed in His blood.

Appendix